THE
URBAN BIKING
HANDBOOK

QUARRY

THE
URBAN BIKING
HANDBOOK

The DIY Guide to Building, Rebuilding, Tinkering with, and Repairing Your Bicycle for City Living

BEVERLY MASSACHUSETTS

QUARRY BOOKS

CHARLES HAINE

First published in the United States of America by
Quarry Books, a member of
Quayside Publishing Group
100 Cummings Center
Suite 406-L
Beverly, Massachusetts 01915-6101
Telephone: (978) 282-9590
Fax: (978) 283-2742
www.quarrybooks.com

Library of Congress Cataloging-in-Publication Data

Haine, Charles.

The urban biking handbook : the DIY guide to building, rebuilding, tinkering with, and repairing your bicycle for city living / Charles Haine.

    p. cm.

ISBN-13: 978-1-59253-695-5 (pbk.)

ISBN-10: 1-59253-695-6 ()

1. Cycling—Handbooks, manuals, etc. 2. City traffic—Handbooks, manuals, etc. 3. Bicycles—Maintenance and repair—Handbooks, manuals, etc. I. Title.

GV1043.7.H25 2011

796.6—dc22

                                                                            2011005061

ISBN-13: 978-1-59253-695-5

ISBN-10: 1-59253-695-6

10 9 8 7 6 5 4 3 2 1

Design: Traffic Design Consultants

Production: Claire MacMaster, barefoot art graphic design

Illustrations: Mario Ferro

Photography: Charles Haine and Drew Bienemann, except for the following: Adam Aufdencamp: page 189 (bottom); © allOver photography / Alamy: page 167 (bottom left); © Anthony Eva / Alamy: page 49 (top left) Dylan Haley: pages 97 and 176; fotolia: pages 36 and 124 (bottom left); istockphoto.com: pages 49 (center top and bottom), 76 (top row), 124 (top left), 125 (left and top right), and 182; Jane ni Dhulchaointigh: page 181; Joe Bell: page 74; © Justin Kase z03z / Alamy: page 49 (top right); Martha J. Retallick: pages 180 and 192; © Michael Kemp / Alamy: page 77 (top right); Michael Mandibergs: page 119 and 166 (left); Rock the Bike: pages 124 (bottom right), 185, and 189 (top); Ryan McFarland: pages 186-187; shutterstock: pages 77 (bottom left), 124 (top right), and 167 (top left); superstock: pages 76 (bottom) and 167 (right); Village Bike Project: page 193; and Zuma: pages 77 (left), 125 (bottom right), 166 (right), 183, and 191

Printed in China

DEDICATION

To my parents for getting me a
bicycle for Christmas when I was 6—
the best Christmas gift ever.

To every mechanic and cycling guru
who has had the patience to teach
me everything I'm lucky enough to
have learned.

To all the folks at the Bicycle Co-op
in Oberlin, Ohio, and the Bicycle
Kitchen in Los Angeles, California,
who've made my life so much richer.

CONTENTS

INTRODUCTION: WHY RIDE BIKES?

We are currently in the middle of a cycling renaissance. In the last few years the do-it-together (DIT) bicycle community and urban cycling have exploded. All kinds of people are riding their bikes for an increasing number of their everyday tasks.

In Los Angeles alone, a city not known for cycling even a decade ago, there are now monthly rides that attract thousands of cyclists riding through the day and night, and a group ride of one sort or another nearly every night of the month. All over the world masses of people are taking to two wheels and powering themselves through their cities like never before.

People are taking an interest in not only owning bikes but also fixing and customizing them themselves. "I'm not a very good mechanic" is probably the thing I hear most often when teaching people how to fix bicycles, as if mechanical skill is something we're born with, like good eyesight or red hair. For years I've volunteered at bicycle education spaces and I've observed that anyone who is interested in learning how to build or fix a bike is able to accomplish her goals. Sometimes it takes longer than we planned, and sometimes the parts aren't immediately available, and often we get really greasy, but it turns out that bicycles are simple to fix.

Once you learn how to fix your own bicycle, two things are likely to happen:

- You'll discover that most things are easy to repair yourself with a simple set of tools.
- You'll find you love your bike more.

The time it takes and the understanding you get from building and repairing your own bicycle creates a bond that lasts. This book can help you learn the basics of how to pick out a good new or used bicycle and fix it up or maintain it yourself. Its mechanical sections are not intended to be exhaustive; there are many books and online resources that can help you rebuild your 3-speed Sturmey-Archer hub or reface your bottom bracket. (Not to mention that it's possible to spend a decade riding and fixing bikes without having to do such tasks.)

This book is designed as a primer for urban cycling and basic bicycle repair. Fixing bikes and the community of people I have found who also love teaching people about the bicycle have enriched my life in many ways, and I hope you are able to get some of the joy I've found on two wheels.

The bicycle is our first means of escape. As children we are completely dependent on our parents or the limitations of where we can reasonably walk to get where we want to go. Then, one magical day, we are granted freedom on two wheels: a bicycle.

The bicycle takes basic human power and augments it, expanding our range of travel. All of a sudden we are no longer limited by our city block or neighborhood; we can go to the next neighborhood over, or even out of town, all under our own power.

As teenagers, we get our driver's license and maybe a secondhand car, and our world opens up even wider, to nearby towns and cities, to work and play opportunities, even to dating people who live farther away. But some of us never transition from the bicycle to the car. And for those of us who do, many go back to the bicycle as our primary transportation.

Cycling, especially cycling in the city, offers everything you might need for transportation. It has a very small carbon footprint, since the only fuel you need to run it is the food you put in your belly and the energy used to make and ship the bike. You never have to look very long for a parking spot, no matter how hip or populous the neighborhood. Instead of sitting in your car in traffic, you whiz right by everyone, and, in many cities, arrive before you would if you had taken a car. When combined with the good public transit systems that exist in virtually every metropolis, bicycling puts the whole city at your command.

Cycling also gives you a feeling of connection to the world around you that is seldom felt in a car. When riding down the street, if you see a friend in a café you can easily stop and chat in seconds, fostering the sort of accidental social contact that helps cities thrive. Not only would you have to look for parking for a car or motorcycle, but you would also likely be going by too quickly to even notice your friend in the café window at all. You also find yourself out in the open air, noticing and appreciating things about your community you wouldn't otherwise see. Gatherings of cyclists at stoplights frequently open up conversations and new friendships.

In the past few decades, dedicated communities of urban cyclists have formed around the globe where folks come together through a common love of cycling as a way of life, not simply a form of recreation.

—Charles Haine

PART I: THE RIDE

CHAPTER 1:
CHOOSING YOUR RIDE

The first question to answer when selecting your bicycle is, what are you going to be doing with your bicycle?

Are you hoping to commute to work on your bicycle every day? Or do you plan to use it on weekends for recreation? Are you anticipating any off-road riding at all, or will you stay on city streets?

Bicycles fall into three main categories: road, mountain, and hybrid.

Road bikes are what many of us still picture when we close our eyes and say "bicycle." They feature larger wheels (27" or 700C); skinny, smooth tires; curvy "drop" handlebars; and large, thin frames. While many find the narrow tire intimidating, with a little practice they are easy to control, and make great platforms for a city bike. Within road cycling there are several broad categories of bikes: the racing bike, the touring bike, and the cyclocross bike. Road bikes typically have the skinniest tires; since these have the smallest area of contact with the road, they have the least "rolling resistance" caused by friction between the tires and the pavement.

Pros: Lightweight, low rolling resistance, fast

Cons: Expensive, can be uncomfortable over long distances

ROAD BIKES can be broken down into several subcategories.

Racing bikes cater every aspect of their design to competitive racing. Frames and components are as light as possible, which generally means there are sacrifices in durability. Racing frames also use an aggressive seating position, with a very steep seat tube that puts the rider's body weight farther forward, and low handlebars so the rider leans over farther, which lowers wind resistance. While beneficial in a race, racing bikes don't tend to be as comfortable for day-to-day cycling. If you have a racing bike you intend to use as a daily commuter, you might consider raising the handlebars and pushing your seat back for more comfort, and be prepared for higher maintenance costs as you put a delicate frame through daily rigor.

Pros: Fast

Cons: Pricey, not very durable

Road/racing bike

Mountain bikes are traditionally heavier than road bikes, with their tubing and components designed to stand up to off-road abuse. They generally feature wide, flat handlebars; a low-slung top tube; and 26" (600 mm) wheels with knobby tires, though 29" (622 mm) wheels are increasing in popularity. Mountain bikes are also notable for their frequent use of suspension to smooth out off-road bumps and drops. In general, suspension should be avoided for city riding. A little skill can help tremendously with avoiding impact. Most of what you'll run across in the city doesn't require suspension, which simply adds weight and decreases the pedaling efficiency of your bicycle. Mountain bikes were invented in Marin County, California, in the 1970s, and exploded onto the bicycle market in the 1980s and 1990s, achieving nearly total domination of the low-priced bicycle market. See page 76 for how to convert a mountain bike for city riding.

Pros: Inexpensive, durable

Cons: Heavy, not well suited to daily or long-distance riding

Hybrids bikes are a strange and wonderful animal. They are designed to combine some of the best attributes of road and mountain bikes: more durable and less expensive than a road bike, but more road friendly than a mountain bike. They take advantage of the economies of scale of mountain bike production to make a very cost-effective bicycle. The design is slightly modified to be better for riding on paved surfaces. Although they are very durable, their main drawback is heaviness. Because they are built on what is closer to a mountain bike platform, they tend to be too heavy for regular city riding over any distance.

Pros: Versatile, durable, inexpensive

Cons: Heavy, jack-of-all trades but master of none

Touring bikes are designed primarily for long bicycle tours. They have a more relaxed seating position and higher handlebars for comfort over long hours on the bike, slightly heavier but more durable frames and components, and mounting points for racks and other gear. Touring bikes make great platforms for city bikes; the riding position is comfortable enough for daily riding, accessories can be conveniently mounted, and they stand up to the rigors of city life. In between racing and touring are club racers, designed for recreational racers, with a less aggressive riding position than a true racer but less weight than a touring bike.

Pros: Comfortable, durable

Cons: Slightly heavier than racing bikes, slower

Hybrid bike

Touring bike

Mountain bike

Cyclocross is an off-road event in which road-style bikes are ridden in off-road courses. They feature lightweight racing frames mounted with mountain bike–style brakes for extreme stopping power, and a short wheelbase for off-road maneuverability. Slightly heavier than road racing bikes, they make excellent city bike platforms because they are durable and nimble with strong brakes. (The short wheelbase makes the overall bike shorter, making weaving through traffic easier.) Their main drawback is a high center of gravity (CoG) or where your weight is centered on the bike. To clear off-road obstacles, they have a high bottom bracket, which moves the rider up off the ground. The high CoG makes the bike harder to lean into a turn—not impossible, but more difficult during high-speed cornering. However, the high bottom bracket also means it's less likely the pedals will hit the ground when cornering steeply or when going over a curb. The cyclocross bike is a very popular frame platform for the city cyclist.

Pros: Very durable, generally light

Cons: High center of gravity, tends to lack rack mounts

Cyclocross bike

Cruiser

Cruisers are one of the few kinds of bike in which form triumphs over function. With giant balloon tires and curved tubes, cruisers are instantly recognizable and are a staple of beach communities and college campuses. Though it is possible to make a nice cruiser, most are poorly made and not designed for longevity. Their upright riding position, though comfortable on short rides, can be very uncomfortable during longer rides and doesn't promote good pedaling efficiency.

Pros: Simple, stylish

Cons: Tend to be very heavy and inefficient

Fixies are single-speed, noncoasting bicycles styled after track-racing bikes, typically with brakes added for city riding. They are lightweight and mechanically very simple, which makes them durable, but they lack the variety of gearing that is useful for climbing and descending hills. If you aren't prepared for the way it feels when your pedals keep moving and you can't coast, you might get thrown over the handlebars.

Pros: Lightweight, stylish, simple, durable

Cons: Not great on hills, might throw you

Fixie

Folding bikes date at least to the Boer War at the turn of the twentieth century, when the British army used folding bikes with rifle mounts. They are fantastic for commuters, especially those who use public transit for part of their commute, or don't have much room to store a bike at home or work. However, all sorts of people find them useful because they are so easy to bring along. They tend to be more expensive because of the added cost of the folding technology; cheaper folding bikes tend to be very fragile and include too many plastic parts.

Pros: Small, easily stored, lightweight

Cons: Expensive or fragile, odd looking

Folding bike

There are also a variety of other specialty bicycles in existence, including tandems, unicycles, tricycles, pedicabs, etc.

While unicycles are primarily recreational devices (and unavoidably associated with circus performers), they are increasing in popularity with off-road cyclists for their extreme versatility. Occasionally you do see unicycle commuters, though generally near a college campus with a large art student contingent.

Tandems, where two or more cyclists are arranged in a line on the bike, are remarkably efficient machines and are able to achieve great speed by taking advantage of putting two cyclists in the same aerodynamic pocket. However, they are unwieldy to operate in cities because of their length, and you rarely see them except in recreational rides in the countryside.

HOW-TO: NEW BIKE VS. USED BIKE

Like many big-ticket items, new bikes sell for a premium price that is about 30 to 40 percent higher than bikes that are barely a few months old. Bicycles that have been made since the 1980s tend to be very durable items, and even bikes dating back to the 1970s or 1960s can still make reliable daily riders with proper maintenance.

A new bike offers a few benefits: you know its history (or lack of one), it is generally covered under at least a 1-year warranty against defects of manufacture, and practically every reputable bicycle shop offers a year of free tune-ups with the purchase of a new bicycle. Whether these benefits are worth the increase in price is a decision every cyclist makes for himself.

A more common route to bicycle ownership is a used bike. Every community offers a variety of outlets for used bikes, from thrift stores to community bike shops to online classified services. Used bikes offer great value, but come with unknowns, such as their previous maintenance history. With most types of bikes, however, a quick visual inspection will reveal if the bike is a lemon.

Examine the frame carefully for any cracks or dings. Though minor scrapes are not a problem, and to some cyclists actually a benefit (someone else has taken care of that emotionally painful first scrape), cracks or major dents in the frame, especially dents or bends that create bulging, should be avoided.

Test the brakes. Before riding an unfamiliar bicycle, give the brakes a quick test by rolling the bike forward and backward while standing next to it and pumping the front and back brakes one at a time; both brakes should bring the bike quickly to a stop.

Take it for a ride. Give the bike a solid test ride—a minimum of twenty minutes, ideally on the terrain you'll be riding in your daily life, up and down hills if you have a hilly area, over rough streets if you live where the paving isn't up-to-date. Do the

gears shift freely without much noise? A little bit of brake squeak is easy to fix (see instructions on page 112), as is a little shifting trouble. If the bike is very difficult to pedal or otherwise feels clunky, trust your gut and walk away from it.

If you are new to cycling, nothing is more important than to test ride a variety of bikes before making a purchase. Bike salespeople can talk for hours about how different frame materials and geometries feel, but until you actually ride them it remains just an abstract theory. Even if you feel you might purchase a used bike, don't be afraid to test ride a few new bikes. Bike shops generally offer the widest selection of bicycles you will find in one place, which will help you make decisions on size, material, and bike type. Also, you might discover the perfect new bike is worth slightly more to you than taking the time to hunt

TUNING IN

While some riders may be skeptical and see the year of free tune-ups as a gimmick to get them back in the shop and more likely to purchase high-margin accessories, it can be a great perk. A brand-new bike will have a natural break-in period as cables stretch, the housing that surrounds the cables compresses, and spokes settle. Bringing the bike back to the shop two or three times for a tune-up in the first year, for free, can help make the bike precisely what you need. Regular tune-ups are also helpful for creating a baseline of what your bicycle is supposed to feel and sound like when riding; then, as it slowly drifts away from perfect adjustment, you will be more likely to notice and know what has changed.

through the numerous used bikes. Even if you purchase a used bike, you will eventually need to purchase new items such as a helmet, a lock, and safety lights, and it is good to become familiar with the bike shops in your neighborhood, and find one where you like the vibe. (Never purchase a helmet used; helmets are discussed in chapter 3.)

Never underestimate the appearance of your bike when making a decision. Human beings are frustratingly shallow, and studies have proven that we use things more often when we think they look cool. Whether your taste is for neon graphics or understated colors, don't be afraid to hold out for a bike that you would ride proudly every day.

SPOTTING STOLEN PROPERTY

It's important to look out for stolen bikes when shopping for a good used ride. If the legal or karmic ramifications of supporting bike theft don't bother you, remember that the bike can also be confiscated at any time. One easy way to spot a stolen bike is if the deal is too good to be true. Shop around online and at local bike shops and you will get a general sense for the value of various bikes and components. A prestigious brand of racing bike with high-end components being sold on the Internet for the price of a low-end cruiser is probably stolen. Also, be on the lookout for individuals who seem to be constantly selling used bikes from their apartment or home

with vague stories about where they got the bikes in the first place. If you see four different posts in the classifieds from the same seller about four different bikes—especially if those posts tell a sob story of broken hearts, cleaning house, or moving on—it's likely the bikes are stolen. While many legit sellers pick up used bikes from police auctions or other avenues, fix them up and sell them, they tend to be upfront with where the bikes came from. If the story is ever sketchy or inconsistent, be wary.

USED BIKE CHECKLIST

- Ensure it's a good fit for you.
- Check all parts thoroughly for cracks or bends.
- Check the braking system.
- Fill the tires and test ride.
- Make sure it's not stolen.

People form strong attachments to their bicycles and can often recognize their own bike months or years later with new tires or other changes. Once when I was working in a bike shop, a man brought in a bike that he had bought in the park for a small chunk of money. Through a wild twist of fate, another customer who happened to be in the shop at the time recognized the man's bike as one that had been recently stolen from him. (The bike's original price was twenty times that of the "small chunk" the new owner paid.) Luckily, the original owner's name was engraved in the bottom bracket of the frame. The original owner got his bike back, but the foolish person who bought the stolen bike lost money. He was also lucky the original owner didn't want to press charges for possession of stolen goods.

BUILDING A BIKE FROM A BARE FRAME

As you gain more experience fixing and tinkering with your bike, you might consider building your ideal bicycle from a bare frame. This is a great experience that will leave you intimately familiar with and proud of your ride.

Building a bike from scratch requires a higher level of technical experience than just tinkering with a bike. You will have to purchase everything you need to build the bike. It will also require some technical savvy to ensure that parts you purchase are compatible with each other.

One irony of the bare frame market is that the price for frames is similar to the price of complete used bikes. This is because the types of frames that are sold alone are usually prestige frames: name-brand frame builders or the high-end frames from mass manufacturers. Though there are cheap frames in the marketplace, they are generally not high quality enough to justify the effort of building a bike from scratch.

Buying a frame also means you won't get a chance to test ride the bike until long after you've purchased it. Thus, it's more important that you are confident about the size of frame you like to ride and the style. A frame that is slightly too big or too small

can be adjusted with seatpost and stem length, but a mountain bike frame will never do when it's a road bike frame that you want. Test ride as many bikes as you can get your hands on to ensure you select the frame that is right for you.

It's important to purchase the frame first: the headset, bottom bracket, seatpost, and brake calipers will need to be sized appropriately to the frame, requiring you to know which frame you have before you get them.

If there is a used bike shop, collective, nonprofit, or co-op in your area, it can be a good idea to get your parts there. They will have parts of different quality and vintage and it will be easy for you to try out a variety of parts that might work for your bike. Nothing is more frustrating than ordering what you thought was the perfect part from the Internet, waiting a week, and then discovering it isn't compatible with your ride.

A more modern bare frame, this one comes with no bottom bracket or headset, meaning you should inspect it thoroughly before purchasing parts to ensure a match.

Luckily, this old frame has its Schwin-sized headset and stem.

Here is a rough shopping list for a geared bicycle:

- Frame and fork
- Headset (1", 1 ⅛", or 1 ¼"; threaded or threadless to match frame)
- Bottom bracket to match frame
- Wheelset (match frame wheel spacing with tires, tubes, and rim strips)
- Derailleurs, chain, and gears
- Shifter levers
- Brake levers
- Brake calipers
- Seatpost to match frame seat tube
- Stem to match headset
- Handlebars
- Grips or grip tape
- Cables and housing
- Saddle

Assembling your bare frame with parts can be a long and involved process, but here is a general outline. Please see the appropriate chapters for more detailed information.

1. Set up your frame in a repair stand, clamping gently to be sure not to damage the frame.

2. Insert the bottom bracket and headset. These often require specialized tools you might not need again, so consider having a professional mechanic install them if you are uncomfortable or don't want to buy or find the tools. However, they are simple to install if you have tool access.

3. Fill the tires with air and attach the wheels. It's important to do this early, to ensure that any slow leaks in the tires and tubes reveal themselves while you complete the rest of the work; this is superior to filling the tires last, before heading out for a ride, and discovering a slow leak 50 miles (80 km) from home.

Doing this step early also offers psychological benefits: your bike starts to look like a bike, which creates momentum for your work.

4. Insert the seatpost and stem.

5. Attach the handlebars, shifters, and brake levers.

6. Attach the brake calipers.

7. Attach the derailleurs and chain.

8. Attach the wheels.

9. Run the cables and housing. Housing should be long enough that the handlebars can move freely, but no longer.

10. Set the brake and derailleur cable tension.

11. Perform a safety check.

12. Test ride and tweak as necessary.

With a very old frame, matching headsets and bottom brackets are helpful because it can be hard to find matching parts.

Campy dropouts, in this case chromed, are among the fine details you might look for when purchasing vintage frames.

GRUPPO

Gruppo is the Italian word for group, and in cycling, gruppo refers to a package of bicycle components all designed to work together flawlessly. Originally, different manufacturers produced all the elements of a bicycle. Your bike might have an Italian frame with French Maillard hubs, Italian Campagnolo derailleur, and Japanese Suntour shifters, and they were all able to work reasonably well together. However, as drive train designs became more complicated, compatibility between brands became more difficult, and individual component manufacturers began to introduce complete lines of parts that could be purchased together as one group.

The first gruppos were high-end racing packages (Record from Campagnolo and Dura-Ace from Shimano are the most famous, but there are many other fine sets out there). Gradually, more cost-effective gruppos were introduced to the market. Mountain bikers tend to refer to gruppos as *groups* or *sets*.

If you are new to building a bike from scratch, consider buying a complete gruppo. They are available on online auction sites, classifieds, or your local bike shop. Buying a gruppo ensures that all the parts you choose work together seamlessly.

However, purchasing a gruppo is not required; my personal bike is a mix of Suntour shifters, Mavic derailleurs and cranks, Dura-Ace brake levers, and Shimano XTR brakes, and it works great.

Gruppos are also one of the ways that bicycle fanatics measure each other's level of obscure knowledge about the history of the various part manufacturers. The highest end parts (Record and Dura-Ace) get the most attention, best engineering, and nicest finishes, and are thus often the most desired. However, because of the sacrifices made to make them lightweight for racing, they are the most fragile. Many cyclists concerned more with durability than pure racing speed settle for middle gruppos, such as Shimano 105. Many touring bikes come kitted out with 105 stock for this reason.

CHAPTER 2: CITY RIDING

Now that you've got your bicycle, there are a few things that every city cyclist needs to know.

SECURITY

Additionally, bike thieves will go anywhere: in the basement garages of apartment blocks, in the courtyards of courtyard apartments, on fourth-floor balconies. If they can't get your whole bike, they will take whatever else they can, including wheels, seats, even pedals.

Currently there are only two styles of bicycle lock worth purchasing: the U-lock and the New York–style chain lock. Both of these are imperfect; with enough time and power tools both can be gotten through.

Bike theft is rampant in all metropolitan areas (and even suburban and rural areas—never assume you are free from it). You should be prepared to spend 20 percent of the value of your bike on security. There is no perfect locking system for a bicycle. The purpose of a lock is to slow down a thief, and hopefully slowing down the thief will make him give up on your bike because of the challenge. That said, no matter how nice a lock you get, if you leave it locked in a bad enough area long enough, the bike—or parts of the bike—will get stolen. Locking up a bike outside overnight is almost never a good idea. While pedestrian traffic might make the two minutes it takes to break a nice lock too risky for a thief at 10 p.m., at 4 a.m. with no one around bike thieves can work undeterred for as long as they need to get access to your ride.

New York-style chain lock, U-lock, and cable lock

Saddle with a DIY anti-theft chain

U-LOCKS

U-locks generally come in a variety of price points based on the hardness of the steel used to make them. Do not scrimp on spending on a lock; cheap locks are easy to break.

The smaller the U of the U-lock, the harder it is for a thief to get leverage, and the more secure the bike. Smaller U-locks are also lighter and easier to carry, making them more convenient—stick one in your back pocket and go.

A simple U-lock doesn't offer any protection for your wheels, however. While you could purchase a long U-lock, take the front wheel off and put it by your rear wheel, and run the long U-lock through the whole assembly, this has several drawbacks. A long U-lock is easier to break, it's inconvenient, and it's messy. In your normal day on a bike you might make anywhere from ten to twenty stops; do you have time to take the front wheel off every time?

NEW YORK–STYLE CHAINS

A better locking solution is one that secures your wheels. One option is the New York–style chain: thick, heavy chains, usually wrapped in an inner tube or cloth sleeve so it doesn't scratch your bike. Running this through both of your wheels, your frame, and a secure area to lock provides very good security. However, these chains are heavy.

The solution I have used for the last decade is locking skewers: replace the quick-release skewers that come with your wheel skewers with custom keyed nuts that only open if you have the keyed wrench. Available from several manufactures, they are lightweight and provide a good measure of security. Though they also aren't perfect and can be opened by a determined thief with time to work and a few tools, they provide enough security that I have ridden the same wheelset since 2000 without them being stolen, despite regularly locking my bike in front of restaurants, bars, and parties on the streets of Los Angeles until late in the evening.

With wheel locks and a small U-lock you can roll up to any parking meter in the city and lock your bike in a matter of seconds. The small U-lock is too small to slide over the top of the parking meter by a thief.

Saddle security is also important: run a length of bicycle chain around your chainstays (the tubes that connect bottom bracket and rear fork ends) and up through the metal saddle rails that hold your seat onto the seatpost to prevent it from being stolen. Many wrap this chain in a tube or electric tape to prevent it from scratching the frame.

PARKING

Be very conscious of where you lock your bike. If all the parking meters, parking signs, trees, and bike racks are full, you may have to get creative. It is acceptable to lock your bike to the security gate in front of a store, but be considerate of the store owners and whether they are likely to open up in the near future. It's bad form to lock up to the inside railings of a handicapped access ramp, since that might restrict wheelchair access, but the outside railings can be safe and secure places to lock your bike.

- Keep in mind what time it is not only when locking up but also when you'll be returning to your bike. Even if the parking spot seems brilliant at 5 p.m. when you stop in for happy hour, if happy hour stretches until 4 a.m., the neighborhood might not feel as secure.

- Try to avoid locking your bike where it might be in someone's way; though made of metal, bikes are delicate creatures. Nothing is as depressing as returning to your locked bike to find it vandalized or crushed by a car.

- Always lock your bike to something secure. If it is locked to a street sign, give it a push to make sure the sign post is solidly embedded in the sidewalk. Countless bikes have been stolen not by breaking the lock but by breaking what the bike is locked to.

THE THINGS THEY CARRY: CHOOSING A BAG

When you are riding around the city, you will need to bring more with you than you can carry comfortably in your pockets. This leads to the question: messenger bag or pannier?

Track bike with rack, loaded with saddlebags

MESSENGER BAGS

Most people riding a bicycle wear a bag with a single shoulder strap. Popularized by couriers, who need to swing the bag around to the front of their body for easy access to its contents, the single-shoulder "messenger" bag has become the de facto method for most cyclists to carry their laptops, books, rain clothes, food, drinks, and everything else one might need for a day (or evening) on the bike.

Many manufacturers make fantastic bags with several features that are key for year-round, all-weather biking:

- Padded shoulder strap
- Quick-release buckles
- Hidden pockets
- Built-in laptop/tablet computer sleeves
- Wet/dry dividers
- Waterproof lining and a large flap to protect against rain or snow

The biggest drawback of the messenger bag is that it's lashed to your back the entire time you are riding, which can lead to misaligned shoulders, back sweat, and back pain. While many cyclists who don't stop as frequently as messengers use bags with two shoulder straps (like a traditional backpack or bookbag), these still have sweat and back-strain drawbacks.

PANNIERS

Panniers are becoming increasingly popular city riding accessories. Originally designed for cycle touring, panniers, sometimes called saddlebags, mount to racks that are bolted onto either the rear triangle or the front fork of a bicycle. They aren't as popular with messengers as they are with commuters, but many city cyclists love panniers.

In addition to sharing many of the features of messenger bags:

- Most are designed for all-season use
- Many feature small pockets for organizing gear

There are a few key drawbacks to panniers. They take longer to put on and take off when you get on and off your bike (10–15 seconds vs. no time at all).

Panniers also slightly alter your bike handling because they add weight to the frame of the bicycle instead of to the rider's back (which is easier to accommodate). This is most evident with front panniers; any weight added to the fork or handle bars makes steering feel twitchier, since small inputs can have big results. The extra weight in the system adds more momentum to your turns; touch the handlebars gently and the steering responds dramatically.

With rear panniers, the extra frame weight affects turning, as the extra low weight pulls you deeper into your lean when you turn. Both are easy to get the hang of, but before your first ride with panniers, take a few circles around a parking lot to get used to them.

Protection for Electronics

Some riders are concerned about stowing electronic gear in panniers, where it is more likely to get knocked around in transit. A laptop on your back is protected not just by the padding of your bag, but also by the natural shock absorption of your legs and knees as your whole body works to keep your head stable while you ride. Lining your panniers with extra padding is a good idea if you plan to carry delicate items in them. On the flip side, in a fall, a laptop in a shoulder bag is more likely to be crushed than one in a pannier.

MESSENGER BAGS

Messenger bags are often used to display personality or political beliefs. For several years in Los Angeles "CVC21202" banners were popular on bags, intended to remind drivers of the state of California's vehicle code, which gives cyclists the full use of a traffic lane when traveling at the appropriate speed.

CHOOSING YOUR FOOTWEAR

Road cycling shoes are designed to be extremely lightweight and have cleats that stick out quite a bit from the shoe and are mounted in the three-screw triangular "look" pattern. These shoes don't make the best city cycling shoe, since they are uncomfortable to walk on when not on the bike.

Your feet provide one of only three contact points with the bicycle, which makes shoe choice extra important.

Mountain bike shoes are a better choice for the city cyclist. In this style, cleats are mounted to mountain bike shoes using the "spd" pattern, which is formed by two small screws next to each other. Ridges run down both sides of the shoe's sole so that the cleat is recessed, which allows you to walk more comfortably in the shoe and also to not worry about scratching floors you might walk on. (Though I always keep a spare pair of shoes at my office to change into, I sometimes forget and leave my mountain bike shoes on all day.)

There are also several styles of touring shoes, and even some touring sandals, that use the two-screw spd recessed cleat pattern that are popular with city cyclists.

Because of their stiff sole and low impact over their lifetime, cycling shoes can have tremendous longevity. My two pairs of cycling shoes are more than a decade old, get used several times a week, and are still in great shape.

For more on shoes, see chapter 3.

PEDALS

Most of the bikes we had when we were young had very simple pedals, which allowed us to push down as we spun our cranks. However, this overlooks half of our potential power: we can also lift up on the pedal through the backstroke, smoothing out our pedal stroke and increasing our road speed with only a slight increase in effort.

To lift the pedals, you need to be attached to your pedals. There are two simple ways to do this: straps and cages or toe clips.

Toe straps are leather or cloth straps that wrap around your foot, held open for you by a cage structure so you can slide your foot easily in or out.

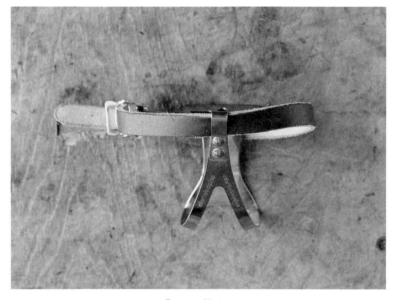

Toe cage with strap

Straps and cages are great for convenience, since you car wear your normal shoe while riding, which is very useful when using your bike in day-to-day life, but they have two main drawbacks. First, your regular shoes might not offer firm enough support for cycling and might get scuffed by the pedals and cages. Second, and more important, in an accident your feet are trapped in the cages; as momentum carries your body forward, your legs can get twisted around because they are stuck in the cages.

Above (Look) and below (SPD), clipless pedals with cleat and shoes

Clips, a newer system of keeping your foot on the pedal that became popular in the 1980s, are also known as clipless or cleats. These require you to wear special shoes with mounting points for cleats that clip into specially designed pedals that have a receiver for the toe clips.

Cleat systems are designed to pop your feet loose in an accident, often allowing you to fly free of a situation. This is generally considered to be the safer option. However, it requires wearing shoes that are dedicated for cycling, since they need to have the built-in mounts of your cleats. Cycling shoes offer other benefits: They are usually very lightweight and have a deliberately stiff sole, so in effect the entire shoe becomes the pedal. Your pedaling force is distributed evenly over your whole foot, which is much more comfortable.

FENDERS

If you live in a city with rain and snow, fenders are an invaluable addition to your bike. Fenders prevent rainwater from splashing up onto your clothes and panniers or bags. Available in a variety of materials, including exotics such as wood and carbon fiber, they tend to be very light and will not significantly affect your riding style.

Plenty of fender clearance for a large tire on this bike.

Be sure to look carefully at the space available between your tires and your frame before purchasing fenders to make sure you have clearance for the fenders to fit. Don't be afraid to consult with the mechanics at your local bike shop and place a custom order to make sure your fenders properly fit your bicycle. Ideally, there should be at least ⅜ inch (1 cm) of space between the tire and the fender so that if something small, like a leaf, gets sucked up in the gap you are still able to keep pedaling.

RIDING IN TRAFFIC

Automobile traffic is a fact of city life. If you are lucky you might live in an area with a lot of cycling or pedestrian-only trails (often created by rails-to-trails initiatives), but for most of us, we ride *with* automobiles.

Most roads were simply not designed with the bicyclist in mind. In fact, when the United States Secretary of the Interior recently suggested that future transportation plans should include consideration of cycling, a national transportation organization publicly criticized even thinking about cycling as a transportation option.

This is in contrast to other areas of the world, where cycling is a vital aspect of transport. In addition to cities famous for cycling, such as Taipei, Amsterdam, and Copenhagen, Trondheim, Norway, has gone to extra lengths to promote cycling. The hill Brubakken is notoriously steep, so this university town installed a very simple bicycle elevator, which operates roughly like a ski lift, letting a cyclist place her foot in a stirrup and get pulled uphill.

Learning to safely and effectively ride your bike in traffic involves learning to share the road that wasn't designed for cycling with other users (drivers, pedestrians) who often are unaware that you have a legal right to share the common resource with them.

Stay off the sidewalk. While you might be tempted to ride on the sidewalk, the proper place to ride a bike is in the street. Sidewalks are filled with pedestrians, dogs, children, and other obstacles that dart about unpredictably and are seldom on the lookout for a vehicle as heavy and fast as a bicycle. It is a danger to everyone for you to ride on the sidewalk. While it's common to ride the last 15 feet (4.5 m) of your trip on the sidewalk from the road to your door or wherever you might lock your bike, I have had enough near misses with toddlers in my neighborhood that I generally walk my bike to the street.

Anticipate traffic. Riding with traffic involves learning to anticipate the flow of traffic and how to interact with it safely and efficiently.

- Generally assume that if someone can turn in front of you, he will turn in front of you.

- Always wait until it is clear that a vehicle is going to come to a complete stop before crossing its path, regardless of who has right of way.

- Many motorists fail to use turn signals when they feel "alone" on the road, causing the most erratic behavior when there are not as many other cars are around.

- Use hand turn signals to let drivers know your intentions.

Know the laws. If you are new to street riding, take a moment to review the laws concerning cycling: your local cycle advocacy group will likely have a summary of laws and ordinances that affect you on their website. For instance, in Los Angeles, every bicycle is treated the same way as a motor vehicle, which means running a red light or riding while intoxicated carries the

same penalty as if done so in your car. However, this also means that you are legally entitled to a lane of traffic, provided you are traveling at a reasonable rate of speed and not obstructing traffic flow.

Every locality is different. In Maine, pedestrians have the right of way on all roads except for interstates. This means that cyclists should defer to pedestrians, and drivers will frequently stop unexpectedly for pedestrians, which can lead to accidents if you aren't paying attention. Get to know the local customs, and if riding in new territory remain extra vigilant.

Some cyclists feel that because they have to maintain momentum, they should be subject to different laws. For instance, stop signs should be treated as yield signs, and stop lights as stop signs, is a common interpretation. While there are many arguments for this (it's much more effort to come to a complete stop at every stop sign for a cyclist), and there are some cities experimenting with this sort of legal framework for cyclists, it's important to follow the rules of your community. If drivers are expecting you to stop at

stop signs in accordance with local traffic laws, they are going to act accordingly. You can place yourself in danger by rolling through them like yield signs when that is not the local custom.

If you feel strongly that the law should be changed, it is safer to organize for the law to be changed than to individually protest it by ignoring it.

In short:

- Know the law, and follow it.

- Remember, to most cars you are invisible.

- Pay attention and try to anticipate how those around you might act.

ASSUME THE BEST,
ANTICIPATE THE WORST

Tensions between cyclists and motorists are nothing new. Cyclists tend to feel very vulnerable on the road; they are out in the city streets with nothing but a layer of clothing and a helmet to protect them from the cars that whiz around them on all sides. Sometimes cyclists get holier than thou: They are riding their bike, doing their part to save the Earth and get in shape, all of which can create a sense of entitlement.

Some biker-drive altercations can be avoided, while others just need to be talked out, face to face.

On the flip side, motorists are in giant steel machines, which have a tendency to cut people off from their surroundings. Additionally, there are more motorists filling the road, and they are moving very fast. They may not see cyclists or may feel that they are "in the way."

Fights between motorists and cyclists are ugly things. In one notorious incident, a car angrily honked at two cyclists who where not getting out of the way fast enough. They flipped off the motorist, who promptly accelerated around them, pulled in front of them and slammed on his brakes, causing both cyclists to go through his rear windshield. Though the driver is now serving time in jail (as he should), remember that the cyclists also flipped him off. Both parties contributed to the situation.

The last fight I got into with a motorist I was on a date. When a large van honked at me I promptly pulled my bike in front of the van and loudly defended myself to the driver, whom I could not see since I was blinded by the headlights.

When I walked to the window, I realized that the driver was a friend of mine. I felt foolish, and no amount of apologizing, both to my date and to my friend, could remove the distinct memory we all had of me standing in the middle of the street attempting to provoke a fight with a driver over a friendly honk. We did not go out again.

This hard lesson shows why I work to always assume the best of people while anticipating the worst. When approaching an intersection, I always anticipate that someone will run a red light, and I act accordingly. But if I am honked at or otherwise rushed, I try to assume it's a friend saying hello, or someone with legitimate reason to be in a hurry, and let it go.

Your first job as a cyclist is to keep yourself alive and do no harm to the image of cyclists. Being polite will serve you well.

HOW-TO: HOP A CURB

Though most of the time you will ride in the street, there will be situations where you need to transition from street to curb and back, such as when first starting a ride or stopping for a snack. Hopping a curb, if not done correctly, can knock your wheel out of true or even ding your rim. Even worse, you could take a hard hit from the saddle, or slide off the saddle and knock your tender bits on your bike frame.

Lift your front wheel off the ground to avoid the curb.

While easiest with a fat mountain bike tire, hopping a curb can be done even on skinny-tired road bikes, but it takes some practice.

1. Slow as you approach the curb, but don't come to a complete stop; some momentum is necessary to hob a curb. Continue to pedal gently through the curb hop.

2. When about to hit the curb, lift up on your front wheel, as if popping a wheelie. Timing is essential; you don't want to go too early or you land too soon. If you can't lift your front wheel easily, practice lifting it off the ground while riding around in circles in a parking lot or grassy field.

3. Let your front wheel land gently on the sidewalk.

4. Keep pedaling forward, or rolling forward on your momentum. Lean all your weight onto the handlebars. If you have toe clips or cages, lift your rear wheel off the ground and swing the back end, pivoting on your fork, onto the sidewalk.

5. Slowly lower your rear wheel.

Congrats, you've hopped your first curb. This move takes some practice, and don't be afraid to spend some time practicing going up and down over a curb until you can do so safely and smoothly.

This maneuver, called "bunny hopping" in mountain bike parlance, is useful in hopping a wide variety of obstacles, including logs, train tracks, and sunbathing snakes by the side of the road.

While continuing to roll forward, lift your rear wheel up off the ground to lessen impact with the curb.

RIDING WITH A GROUP

While cycling, especially commuting, is often a solo activity, riding with a group of other cyclists offers many benefits.

The benefits include:

- A friendly spirit of competitiveness often makes us ride a little faster than we might on our own.
- We tend to venture farther than we might solo.
- Sharing something so enjoyable with others is a great feeling.

Whether you are commuting with coworkers, participating in a fitness training ride, or conquering the night on a bar crawl with friends, there are additional considerations for riding in a group beyond what you need to consider as a solo cyclist.

Walk (ride) the line. When riding in a group, riding in a straight line is important. On solo rides it's fun to weave back and forth a little bit. Doing this in a group ride means paying extra attention to where the riders are around you in order to

ensure you don't knock them off their bikes.

Anticipate en masse. Anticipate where you will be coming to a stop and slow down gradually if possible; sudden braking in a group of cyclists can mean a messy accident. Before you begin, perhaps mention the importance of announcing one's intentions, and that it's easier to speak to other cyclists than to motorists.

Tune in to obstacles. It's considered polite to point out obstacles and obstructions in the road when you see them first; this is especially important on racing rides, where a pack of riders with skinny tires are constantly on the lookout for anything that might cause a flat.

GETTING DOORED

If you ride too close to parked cars, eventually someone is going to open her door without looking and you are going to get doored.

There most common type of dooring occurs when the driver opens the car door into your path, and you ride right into it. A less common type of dooring involves an even more inattentive driver: the car door flies open while you are riding next to it, knocking you off your bike and into the nearest lane of traffic.

Both of these situations can cause tremendous damage to you, your bike, and the car.

- Always keep at least an arm's length between you and any parked car, even if this puts you in a lane of traffic. Drivers in the street are more likely to notice and avoid you than drivers getting out of their car.

- Always be vigilant around parked cars: any door might swing open at any moment.

SCRAPES AND CRASHES

Though it doesn't happen often, you *will* fall off your bike. It happens to everyone, and while you should do everything you can to avoid it, you shouldn't give up cycling just because every once in a while you fall off. We fall down walking sometimes, too, but that doesn't mean we should all resort to motorized scooters.

In the unfortunate event you are hit by a car or are present when a friend is, there are several things to keep in mind:

If you are coherent enough, make sure you get the license plate number. Once, when I was hit by a car, the driver got out of her car to talk to me, then refused to show me her ID, jumped back into her car, and drove away. I was too dazed by the accident to get her plate number, but multiple bystanders volunteered it.

Get the contact information of as many witnesses to the accident as possible.

Do not hesitate to call an ambulance immediately, especially if you feel nauseous or dizzy, are bleeding heavily, or were hit in the head. We are vulnerable out there on our bicycles and getting proper medical attention if needed is a must.

If it is a small fall with only light cuts, clean the wound immediately. This is the reason many road cyclists—men and women—keep their legs shaved; it's not for aerodynamics, but to make it easier to clean dirt and gravel out of their wounds with minimal pain after a fall.

For simple injuries or soreness, try to ride it off once you are patched up. It's important to get back on the bike as soon as possible to avoid building up any psychological barrier to riding your bike again.

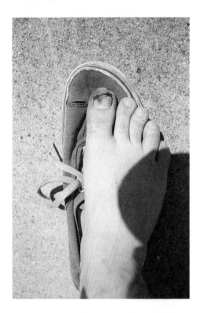

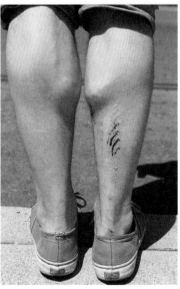

CHAPTER 3:
URBAN OUTFITTING

When we were kids, we could jump on our bikes with whatever we had on and ride down the street to our friend's house and play all day in the same outfit. Unfortunately, as we grow older and we have to attend school, work, and social events, we have to become more conscious of what we wear and what we carry, and in general outfit ourselves for not just a cycling lifestyle but a grown-up cycling lifestyle.

All lifestyle choices come with overhead costs. Unless you are capable of hour-long meditations (and more power to you if you are), traveling by public transit calls for some overhead in the books, newspapers, e-readers, and wireless devices that you buy to keep yourself entertained. Traveling by car has overhead not only in gasoline, maintenance, repair, and parking (never mind the cost of the car itself) but also in physical therapy and gym memberships for spending such a chunk of your life sitting in one place.

While it might seem like a lot of kit, cycling has a fairly low overhead, and most of the tools and clothing you purchase will last for years or decades. Additionally, you can buy this stuff slowly over time. It helps you ease the pain of spending the money, of course, but it also gives you a chance to evaluate what really is useful to you.

BIKE CLOTHING

You can ride a bike wearing just about anything, but once you are riding regularly you will probably discover that a few modifications in your wardrobe can greatly benefit life on a bicycle.

Mogwai wears a traditional
cycling cap and racing jersey.

Layering is essential for cycling. Whether your day starts at 6 a.m. or 4 p.m., the temperature will change throughout the day in ways you may not have noticed when using a car. It's best to wear a few layers so that once you are riding, and your body warms up, you can strip off a layer or two. If you go for a lunch ride or leave work in the afternoon heat, you'll probably want to strip down to your base layer T-shirt, button-up, or tank, but if you are staying out late, you'll need your top layers again. All of this requires some place to store these layers while you ride (see The Things They Carry: Choosing a Bag, page 30).

TOPS

Here are a couple of options to layer with.

Jerseys

Originally, bicycling jerseys were made of wool for its breathability, durability, and odor-prevention qualities. However, as with many other clothing, wool jerseys have largely been replaced in the marketplace with a variety of synthetic jerseys with racing or other logos printed all over them.

The jersey has a few primary benefits.

1. It's long in the back, which is helpful because you tend to be bent over on a bicycle and it will protect your decency.

2. It often has very long zippers at the neck, making it easy to adjust for body temperature.

3. It has wide, deep pockets on the bottom of your back, which is an ideal place to stash small essentials like your cell phone or a banana.

Since I ride to work and parties on my bike, I tend to stick with simpler, logo-free wool jerseys, still available from several manufacturers. They can look quite stylish when worn over a button-up shirt, and they last forever.

Jackets

For cold and/or snowy weather, most riders pile on the layers, topping off with a heavy jacket or coat. Be sure to find a coat that allows you the freedom of movement you need, and that has arms long enough to cover all the way to your hands when you are stretched all the way forward, as you will be on your bike. Most winter coats actually don't fit that well on a bicycle because of shorter sleeves, and they are too tight across the shoulders to give you enough range of motion while cycling.

Puffy jackets and parkas are usually too bulky to comfortably operate your bicycle and to safely be able to look around and monitor traffic. In colder climates, riders start with one or more layers of long underwear beneath a thick winter jersey and then a water- and windproof outer shell. Combined with thick winter cyclist gloves, designed with thin fingers to give good braking control, you can stay warm even on the coldest days once your body warms up from the exercise.

BOTTOMS

The body has three main areas of contact with a bicycle: feet, hands, and bottom. About 50 percent of your weight rests on the saddle, with the rest distributed between your feet and hands. It is vital that this high-friction point of contact is dressed well.

Cycling Shorts

Racers wear dedicated spandex cycling shorts with a built-in padded chamois lining, which are designed to be worn without underwear. The chamois lining is great for wicking away moisture and also provides a small amount of padding.

Warning: The first time you try on cycling shorts, you will feel ridiculous. And that's all right. But, once you move beyond that, they will make you much more comfortable on the saddle. Also, because of their low wind resistance, your legs spin freely back and forth with little drag, and there are no pant legs to flap in the wind.

Most city riders don't consider cycling shorts to be practical for day-to-day riding. Mountain bike shorts, which have the same padded lining but are baggy and styled like cargo shorts, are a popular alternative for city riding.

You may consider wearing spandex cycling shorts with another pair of pants or shorts over them. You'll get the best of both worlds: all the comfort of cycling shorts without looking like a superhero.

Cycling Pants

Cycling is tough on pants; even the skinniest jeans occasionally get caught up in the chain, and if your pants are baggy at all you will need to cuff the leg on the same side as your chain to prevent it from getting tangled in your drive train. The knees of your pants get stretched quickly, and your lock pocket—if you have one—often wears out from the added weight.

Many riders have a "dress-up" pair of pants for walking around the neighborhood, and their cycling pants, which are primed for abuse. In some cities or neighborhoods, it's not uncommon to cuff or cut off cycling pants into knickers in order to avoid drive train hassle.

Specialty cycling pants are made by several manufacturers, which feature a higher waist in back; reinforced, roomier knees; and tapered, slightly short legs. These are a great investment, but also tend to be pricey.

When wearing trousers or cycling pants, you can wear your normal undergarments instead of cycling shorts, but be prepared to wear through them pretty quickly; they aren't usually designed for the high level of friction of your legs swinging back and forth on the saddle.

The bicycle commuter has myriad options available to him in terms of gear. Clothing that does double-duty as functional and street-friendly is ideal.

Only the most devoted—or devoutly car-free—will bear the brunt of winter on their bike.

The things you carry on your bike might need to be carried off the bike as well; consider lightening your load when packing panniers for the day.

There's more than one way to beat the rain when you're on your bike.

Skirts

The key element in riding in a skirt is being conscious of the potential to reveal yourself and taking necessary steps to cover up without restricting your movement. It's possible, and very enjoyable, to wear medium-length to short skirts on a bicycle. One of my good friends rides in a skirt about 3 inches (7.6 cm) above the knee, and very flouncy, which she says feels great to ride in on a summer's day.

If the skirt is flouncy you can wear a pair of running shorts underneath. While truly short skirts are hard to wear on a bike, a shortish skirt with a bit of spandex in the material can be great to ride in. However, anything that is cut narrowly and has no flex is likely to rip.

Mid-length skirts and longer don't usually need any special undergarments, but with exceptionally long skirts I recommend 1980s-style skirt clips or tying the skirt up to prevent it from getting caught in the chain.

If you are a frequent skirt wearer you might considering getting a step-through frame instead of one with a high top bar, since the high bar can interfere with many skirts.

As my friend Kat puts it: "Nothing feels as free and wonderful, and I feel most powerful, wearing a skirt riding a bike. Wearing a skirt is a big part of my identity as a lady, and if I couldn't wear a skirt while riding my bike it would feel oppressive to me and I wouldn't ride a bike at all."

Shoes

Although formal cycling shoes were discussed in chapter 2, they deserve a little extra attention. Many casual city cyclists wear street shoes when they ride. There are some basic considerations when choosing street shoes to wear on the bike.

Riding in flip-flops or any sandal is a bad idea. You can do it for short rides to the corner store or to a BBQ, but you don't want your toes uncovered so close to spinning gear teeth and chains. It's a recipe for disaster.

Additionally, flip-flops don't tend to offer much foot support, which can become uncomfortable pretty quickly. Although it's important to wear comfortable shoes while cycling, shoes with stiffer soles will allow you to push down with your whole foot when pedaling, instead of just the small surface where your foot meets the pedal.

Otherwise, any shoe with a good stiff sole will work well. Breathability is important; your feet will sweat a lot while cycling. Wearing shoes or boots with heels while riding a bike might seem counterintuitive, especially since their slick soles slide around on pedals, but it can make riding easier, since the heel can be wrapped around the pedal for extra traction. Though fun around the city, heels aren't a good idea for longer rides.

Shoelaces seem to be almost magnetically attracted to your drive train. To avoid constantly having to replace your laces, there are a few popular tactics. Most cycling shoes come with shorter laces or some sort of lace covering system. If you aren't riding in cycling shoes, tie your laces so the knot isn't in the center of your foot but actually off to one side, then tuck the excess lace into your shoe next to your foot.

GLOVES

Wearing gloves on a bicycle is usually a good idea, since you'll be resting some of your weight on your hands and they will get fatigued and often blistered without some sort of covering.

Unless you are riding a fixie or a coaster brake bike, you are going to need your hands to operate the brake levers. For this reason, most cyclists wear fingerless gloves, which allow for a more solid grip and control of their brakes.

If you opt to ride in a pair of noncycling gloves, such as gardening gloves or even mittens, be sure to test your braking a few times, including a few passes from full speed to a dead stop. If you can't get a safe grip, cut at least your index and middle fingers off the glove. Your hands should never slip off the brake handles.

Gloves should have a nice thick pad on the palm for comfort, and should be made from a durable material, because the constant gripping and twist they undergo tears through materials pretty quickly.

Keeping Your Hands Warm

Because your hands are in the direct path of the wind, on a chilly day they will often feel unbelievably cold. Your hands are tough little creatures, however, and can withstand the elements quite well. If it's not cold enough for you to get frostbite, it's more important to sacrifice a little comfort and have slightly cold fingers and braking control than to risk not being able to stop your bike when you need to. Cyclist-specific fingerless gloves are common in warm weather; in colder weather winter cycling gloves with thinner finger pads still give you braking control and are a great option.

One of the hidden benefits of cycling gloves is a small, fuzzy pad on the back of the hand that can stretch all the way across the back or just cover your thumb. Manufacturers try many different euphemisms for this section ("comfort pad," "fuzzy area," etc.), but it has one purpose: snot pad.

While riding, you suck in lots of air and breathe hard; you are going to generate a lot of mucus. Cyclists get rid of this by "snotting": hold one nostril down with a finger, turn your head to the side, give a quick peek to make sure there is no one behind you, then exhale rapidly through your nose. Repeat for the other nostril.

Snotting usually leaves your nose a little bit drippy, and you use the snot pad to clean it up.

Before you recoil in horror, think about it. From an ecological standpoint, why use a tissue, which had to be shipped to you and now needs to be thrown away? Snotting is well accepted in the cycling community, and you will see riders snotting who, off the bike, would never do anything even the slightest bit uncouth.

SUNDRIES

Hats or caps. Most of your body heat escapes through your head, so on chilly days a hat is great for cycling. There is a wide variety of cycling caps available that fit easily under a helmet and provide a small amount of comfort against the elements.

Scarves. Scarves are popular with some cyclists, but it's important to arrange them properly. A long dangling scarf can get wrapped around your back wheel, which could cause your rear wheel to freeze, and can even strangle you. Try to ride with scarves that fall no longer than your torso. A tube-style neck warmer can be even more effective since it's easy to pull up over your face for warmth and stays securely in place.

Ear fairings were briefly made in the 1980s to keep ears warm and cut down on the aerodynamic drag of your ears. Nobody wears ear fairings.

Lock holders. Many cyclists purchase a lock holder or a pack worn around their waist for carrying their lock. A back pocket is a convenient place to hold a lock, but it does tend to stretch out over time.

Leggings and armings. These accessories are popular with cyclists of both genders. Generally made of spandex, they can be easily slid on or off your arms or legs throughout the day to help the transition through a variety of weather conditions, adding or removing warmth as needed without wearing extra layers.

RAINGEAR

Rain is considered by many to be a reason not to ride their bike, but if you get over the initial 30 seconds of discomfort, riding your bike in the rain is a ton of fun.

The essential raingear every cyclist should have is the hooded rain jacket. Lightweight and waterproof, often with ventilation in the armpits, rain jackets should cover your lower back with flaps to allow ventilation for your body heat without letting the rain in.

Most are designed to be small and packable so you can stick them into your bag and forget about them when the sun's out, and they'll be there waiting for you when it rains again.

Some cyclists wear rain pants as well, but others consider them too cumbersome and skip them altogether, since their legs tend to be working hard enough to keep warm even in a chilly drizzle.

Almost all messenger bags and panniers offer some waterproofing, and some messenger bags are even divided into waterproofed sections so you can store your wet raingear in your bag without getting the other items stored in your bag wet while you're not on the bike.

Rain covers for your shoes and helmet are also a good idea, but not as essential.

My typical outfit for a day of city riding is a variation on the following:

- Sneakers with stiff soles
- Jeans that are skinny enough not to get bound up in the chain
- Cheap underwear or cycling shorts
- Button-up shirt with a wool jersey
- Gloves
- Scarf or jacket stuffed into the bag or tied carefully to the frame

TOOLS

Basic bicycle maintenance can be accomplished by anyone with the inclination and a few basic tools. It's a good idea to carry a simple tool kit when you ride, either stowed in your bag or in a zippered pouch on your bike, often under the saddle.

Components of a patch kit

Multi-tool hex set

A quality tool can last a lifetime if used correctly. Often it's worth it to spend a little extra money on a tool that is properly constructed. However, most tools are very easy to break if used improperly; be sure to learn its proper use before putting it into action.

METRIC ALLEN WRENCH SET

Allen wrenches are six-sided wrenches. You get them for free when buying semidisposable furniture from Swedish mass-market charitable retailers.* Six sides is not the ideal; originally the design called for four sides, but the Ford Motor Company had a patent on the four-sided "key" wrench, so we today live with a six-sided Allen wrench.

It's true: IKEA is registered as a charity. Look it up!

Most modern bicycles are designed so the Allen wrench is the only tool you need for many repairs. I own two sets of multiple wrenches, both of which fold up into neat packages. The small set has a 3-, 4-, and 5-mm wrench along with a flathead and a Philips head screwdriver and goes with me everywhere in my messenger bag. At home I have a larger kit, which starts even smaller at 2.5 mm and goes up to 8 mm.

Many items on your bike require Allen wrenches:

- Seatpost binder bolts
- Stems
- Some brake calipers
- Most derailleurs
- Water bottle cages
- Newer cranks

For little tweaks, especially seat height, carry a small Allen wrench kit.

REQUIRED TOOLS

❏ Metric Allen wrench set
❏ Patch kit
❏ Tire levers
❏ First aid kit
❏ Frame/bag pump
❏ Chain lube
❏ Rags (used)

Frame/bag pump

Chain breaker tool

PATCH KIT, TIRE LEVERS, AIR PUMP

You'll need a patch kit when you get a flat tire. The kit contains patches, rubber cement, sandpaper, and (of course) instructions. A properly patched tire is stronger than it was before, which may or may not have inspired Hemingway's line that we all break, but later we hope we're stronger in the broken places. Self-adhesive patches are available, too. Don't get them.

Tire levers are plastic or metal levers that allow you to get your tire off the rim so you can access the tube for patching, or to swap out your tires altogether.

A frame/bag pump is a pump that is small enough to carry with you, for when you need to patch a flat on the road. These take forever to fill up your tire, so they aren't too effective at home, but in a pinch, it's better to have a pump than not.

FIRST AID KIT

Although not technically a tool for your bike, it's a really good idea to keep a small first aid kit with some bandages, antiseptic, painkillers, and tweezers to clean up your wounds.

CHAIN LUBE AND RAGS

You need to lube your chain every few weeks, or after any rainy or snowy ride. Chain lube comes in a variety of forms and formulas and with a variety of ingredients, dry vs. wet, waxy vs. silicone, and too many other varieties to count. Choose one style and be consistent; mixing lubes can lead to a gunky chain. You'll need the rags to wipe up excess lube and grease, but you don't need to go to an auto supply shop and buy a bag of "shop rags." An old cut-up T-shirt or pillowcase does the job. Just be sure and wash them in a separate load from the rest of your laundry; the grease can infiltrate everything you wash it with.

CHAIN BREAKER

The chain breaker is a wondrous tool that allows you to take the chain apart and put it back together. It is delicate, however, so make sure that you and anyone you loan it to knows how to use it properly.

In addition to breaking a chain to replace the chain or your derailleurs, a chain breaker is also useful because it can put a chain back together, so if you break a link on the road you can use the chain breaker to take the bad link out and put your chain back together for the ride home (see page 157).

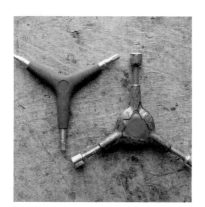

Three-way box wrench/"Y" hex tool

Nipple wrenches

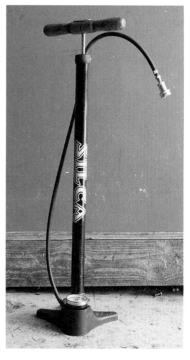

Floor pump

BOX WRENCHES

Many people are familiar with adjustable wrenches, which are great for very basic operations. However, it is difficult to maintain a snug fit when applying any real pressure, making it likely to slip, stripping out the nut. As often as possible, use a box-end wrench, which wraps the nut completely. It provides the most secure fit possible as you adjust the nut.

Most nuts on a bicycle can be tightened with a few simple box-end sizes, so a box-end three-way tool, which includes a 6-, 8-, and 10-mm wrench, is a popular option. Box wrenches are most often used on older-style seatpost binders, stems, brake and derailleur cable clamps, and brake and shift levers.

NIPPLE WRENCH

A nipple wrench allows you to tighten or loosen the spokes of your wheel. While some uses for the nipple wrench, such as wheel construction and truing, are not covered in this book, we show you later how to do a simple wheel truing on the road without a truing stand (page 140). A nipple wrench, when correctly sized, is vital to keeping your wheels running straight.

FLOOR PUMP

Though not absolutely essential, all cyclists should consider a floor pump, and not one of the cheap ones from the toy section. A good floor pump, designed for bicycles, will fill your tire to proper pressure quickly and efficiently. Your tires naturally lose about 10 percent of their pressure a week. A floor pump, used once or twice a week, or every time you ride, can made a world of difference.

INESSENTIAL TOOLS THAT ARE COOL TO HAVE

- ❑ Pedal wrench
- ❑ Fourth hand tool
- ❑ Flat wrenches
- ❑ Crank puller/crank bolt wrench

Fourth hand tool

FOURTH HAND TOOL

The fourth hand tool is designed to hold the brake cable taut while you are adjusting your brakes (see page 111). Some mechanics swear by them, while some never use them at all.

Flat wrenches/cone wrench

FLAT WRENCHES

Flat wrenches are open-ended wrenches with a flat profile, so they can be used with flat nuts, which are common with bearing systems. It is not an essential tool, but if you want to properly repack your hubs (one of the most fun things to do with your bike, see page 145) you'll need some sort of flat wrench.

Crank puller/crank bolt wrench

CRANK PULLER/CRANK BOLT WRENCH

To remove the cranks from your bike, which gives you access to the bottom bracket system—the area of the frame that contains the bearings that allow your cranks to rotate—and allows you to change out your cranks, you need to use a crank puller, and sometimes a crank bolt wrench.

While the most common reason to remove your cranks is to gain access to the bottom bracket, you might also want to replace your cranks for either technical reasons (changing the number of gears or crank length) or aesthetic ones (pretty cranks do exist).

The crank puller works by threading one cuff into the crank arm, then driving the center threaded rod through the cuff into the bottom bracket, pushing the crank off the bottom bracket spindle. Only do this when you have already removed whatever nut is holding the crank on, using a crank bolt wrench if necessary, or else you'll strip the crank.

Pedal wrench

PEDAL WRENCH

The pedal wrench is designed for taking your pedals off and on. While this can be done with a standard open-ended wrench, the pedal wrench provides extra leverage. I change my pedals a few times a week (from clip-in spd pedals for long rides to touring pedals for commuting/socializing), so owning a pedal wrench is super convenient.

SAFETY

Safety on your bike is contingent on three controllable factors and one uncontrollable factor. The three factors in your control are:

- **Ensuring that your bicycle is in proper working order**

- **Making sure you have the right safety accessories (lights and a helmet, etc.)**

- **Riding safely**

The uncontrollable factor is the world at large. There are cyclists killed every year who did everything right and just happened to be in the wrong place at the wrong time. While frightening, especially because you are so exposed on a bicycle, it is an unavoidable part of life. Hunting and gathering both involved risks for early humans; chariot driving was very risky for the ancient Greeks and Romans; trains and cars have their share of accidents; and so riding a bicycle is no exception. (And even if you don't leave the house, who knows when a comet or out-of-control truck might come crashing through your ceiling or walls?)

HELMETS

Helmets are designed to compress on impact; they take the force of the hit so that your head doesn't have to. As such, you get only one big hit per helmet; after one serious accident, you need to replace your helmet with a new one (never a used one). Even if there are no evident cracks or damage, it is possible that the undercarriage of the helmet was structurally damaged and would not protect you in a second crash. Combine this with the fact that helmet material ages very rapidly in sunlight, and you can see why a used helmet is always a bad idea.

- Find a helmet that is both comfortable and you don't think makes you look too dorky. You are more likely to wear a helmet and have it save your skull if you don't feel totally ridiculous wearing it.

- Proper helmet fit is fairly snug, but not so tight it's uncomfortable. Shake your head from side to side. If the helmet moves separately from your skull, it's not fitted properly and won't protect you adequately.

WHY SHOULD YOU WEAR A HELMET?

Also, unlike motorcycling, where the average speed is around 65 mph (100 km per hour) or more, most cyclists tool around their neighborhood going less than 20 mph (32 km per hour). For a quick ride down the street to meet a friend at a coffee shop, many would argue that a helmet is unnecessary. Even on that short ride to the coffee shop, it is possible to be hit by a car and go through a windshield, or fall and hit your head on the curb, in which case you'll wish you had a helmet on.

- Follow the rules or laws that govern your area. If helmets are required, wear a helmet.

- A helmet is always a good idea, especially if you will be on the bike for any significant length of time, or riding on any larger or busy roads. It's also worth mentioning that many lawyers won't take your case if you were injured while cycling if you weren't wearing a helmet.

- A helmet is absolutely essential if you are mountain biking, and maybe even more safety gear, such as shin and knee pads.

That helmets are a controversial subject is surprising to some people outside the cycling community. Who could argue with helmets, other than surly teenagers rebelling against their parents?

It turns out there are well-reasoned arguments both for and against wearing a helmet when you ride. Independent studies have observed that riders without helmets tend to ride more conservatively and have fewer accidents and that drivers tend to give a wider berth to cyclists without helmets (although you can't rely on all drivers to act this way).

LIGHTS AND REFLECTORS

By law all bikes are required to have reflectors: front, back, and on the pedals. Reflectors provide a very limited amount of safety, as they only reflect light that is already headed in that direction. It's far more important to have an emissive light source on your bike, ideally two, to announce your presence to others on the road and increase your safety.

Most city ordinances require that all bikes have lights, as they are moving vehicles, which requires illumination. However, most bicycles are not sold with lights included or attached. (Think about it: what if when buying a car or a motorcycle, you were required to make extra purchases to make your new vehicle legal?)

Even in well-lit city areas, lights are essential to help drivers see you. Drivers are already on the lookout for red taillights and white headlights, and are more likely to see you and avoid hitting you if you have emissive lights in the colors they are looking for. A blinking red light is especially effective since it extends battery life (it's only on half the time, or less) and people are more likely to notice things that change than things that are constant.

LED lights. LED lights are the most common and come in a variety of styles. The bare minimum you should consider for city biking is a red blinker in back and a white blinker or constant light in front. No matter how they are mounted, lights are easy to steal, so light

manufacturers have made them especially easy to take off and on your bike with the idea that you will remove them whenever you aren't riding. Though it might initially seem like a hassle, it's a very easy habit to get into to keep your lights in your pocket or bag and quickly put them on whenever going out for a ride.

Generator lights. Generator lights are popular in Europe and increasing in popularity worldwide. They use a small generator to power the lights, saving battery expenses. The generator, typically attached to the rim like a brake or built into a hub, takes advantage of the spinning of the wheel to generate electricity. In doing so, it creates additional drag, which slows you down slightly. It's a small trade-off to make to power your own lights and never require battery purchases (with their toxic chemicals) for your bike again. Because of the racing-dominated nature of the bike industry, they haven't always been popular, but they appear to be making a comeback.

A small cylindrical flashlight can easily be attached to your handlebars with an old inner tube. Take a 6-inch (15 cm) piece of tube and cut a hole in either end, then place the flashlight on your bars and hook one end of the tube onto the flashlight. Wrapping the tube around the handlebars, hook the other end to the other end of the flashlight, and you are ready to go. If the flashlight moves around too much, you can use another piece of old tube wrapped around the flashlight body to hold it in place.

THE SAFETY CHECK

Testing your brake levers in the Bicycle Pantry

After doing any repair on my bicycle, I always do a quick safety check before going on a ride.

This ensures that all the components are in proper working order and that I'm going to have a safe bicycle that performs as expected while I'm on the road.

1. Lift the front and rear wheel off the ground one at a time and gently let it fall to the floor. Listen for anything that sounds loose or jangly, and investigate it.

2. One at a time, grab each wheel and push it side to side within the frame. This will let you know if the wheel is mounted properly (if it is, it shouldn't move at all in its dropouts) and if the bearings are properly adjusted.

3. Push the bike forward and backward on the ground, closing and opening the brakes one at a time. Each brake should bring its wheel to a complete stop quickly and easily and without resistance.

It never hurts to take a quick spin around the block before taking your bike out for a longer ride, to make sure it's in proper working order and to give anything that is about to break a chance to break while you are still at home near your tools.

CHAPTER 4: CUSTOMIZATION

Humans love to make things their own. We modify our homes, we decorate our tools, we even change our bodies with tattoos. Once you have purchased or inherited your bicycle, there are still a ton of things you can do to make it your own.

Extra cycle, customized; stepladder optional

In order to be profitably mass-produced, most bicycles are aimed at satisfying most of the needs of a large number of people. This is great, since it gets more bicycles into the world, but also means that it can be very hard to find a bicycle that does everything you need it to, fits you perfectly, and reflects your personality.

Most of the customization in this section is about mastering the basic skills that will allow and inspire you to do more elaborate work on your bike. From the simplest (swapping out parts) to the most elaborate (getting out the welding equipment), modifying your bike is reasonably easy and very fun.

GETTING IN THE SADDLE

It seems counterintuitive, but a good saddle is a hard saddle.

Down at the base of your buttocks you have two sit bones, which were evolutionarily developed to support the weight of the upper half of your body while sitting comfortably for long periods of time.

Because soft saddles intuitively seem like they should be more comfortable, novice cyclists tend to desire them. When you sit on a suitably stiff saddle that fits you correctly, your sit bones rest on firm surfaces that lift the rest of your body up off the seat.

If your saddle has too much padding, your sit bones sink into the saddle, and the padding actually puts pressure on the area surrounding your sit bones, including the soft tissue in between your sit bones. This leads to numbness and tingling and other uncomfortable situations.

Look for a saddle with a width that is wide enough to comfortably support your sit bones. If your saddle is too narrow for your sit bones to gain good purchase, get a wider saddle. When saddle shopping, don't be afraid to sit on the saddle in the middle of the shop; you'll be able to feel right where your sit bones sit and get a sense of its comfort.

Saddle with a shock absorber

Track bike saddle

Old-school low quality saddle

Special saddle for going easy on the soft parts

HOW-TO: SET YOUR SEAT HEIGHT AND ANGLE

There is no such thing as perfect seat height, and you do not need a professional to set it for you. You just need to tune in to your body. Depending on how flexible your legs are feeling, how thick your pants or shoe soles are, and what kind of riding you are going to be doing, your seat height might change day to day. Here are general instructions for adjusting your seat for a comfortable ride.

1. Find a way to stand your bicycle upright. Have a friend secure it by placing the front wheel between his or her legs and holding the handlebars, if possible. If not, lean against a wall with one hand while sitting up in the saddle.

2. Put your feet on the pedals and pedal backward.

3. The ideal position is where your leg is almost all the way extended, but not quite, at the bottom part of your stroke. If your leg is all the way extended at the bottom of your pedal stroke, lower your saddle. If your leg is not coming close to extending all the way, raise your saddle.

4. To lower or raise your saddle, loosen the quick-release lever or Allen bolt at the base of your seatpost and gently raise or lower the seatpost to where your leg is in its ideal position at the bottom of the pedal stroke.

Everyone's body is different, and many find saddles that are tilted slightly, either nose up or nose down, more comfortable. To set the angle of your seat, go for a ride, and stop occasionally to tip the front of your saddle gently up or down. Many cyclists find a slight amount of nose-up on the saddle most comfortable, since it rests their body back on their sit bones.

Hard leather saddles are increasingly popular with cyclists for their longevity and aesthetics. I've been riding mine for a solid decade and it still looks almost new and is perfectly comfortable and broken in to my body. Hard leather saddles do require a break-in period to accommodate your specific body shape, but once they are broken in they serve you well.

Many saddles feature an anatomical cutout in the middle to prevent any pressure at all being exerted on the soft tissue between your sit bones. While this might not be necessary with a properly fitted saddle, you may prefer a little padding for your sit bones.

Traditionally, women's saddles are wider across the back, to accommodate their more widely spaced sit bones.

Wrap electrical or cloth tape around your bike's seatpost to mark your ideal seat height, in case you have to remove the saddle.

HANDLEBARS

Your handlebars give you control of your bike, and come in two common flavors, flat straight bars for mountain bikes, and curvy drop bars for road bikes. Other varieties are increasing in popularity.

Road bars

Track bars

Your handlebars should be wide enough that you can keep your hands comfortably about as far apart as your shoulders; this allows for easy breathing and increased comfort.

Drop bars. This style is common on road bicycles. They have a flat top area and twist around before dropping down and looping back, hence their name. They are designed to give you a variety of hand positions for different riding situations and to prevent hand fatigue when on a long bicycle ride.

Hand placement on drop bars:

- Use the flats on top when are you riding slowly.
- Use the drops when riding fast.
- Pull up on the extension pieces when climbing, for more leverage.

Flat bars. This style is typically associated with mountain bicycles. They tend to be wider than drop bars to give you more leverage when climbing an incline, but do not offer the variety of hand positions that many riders appreciate.

Moustache bars. This style is less common, but is growing in popularity, because they offer many hand positions similar to drop bars, but you don't have to reach down quite as far to reach the climbing position. This makes the riding position more comfortable, though it sacrifices aerodynamics.

Drop bars and moustache bars are designed to be wrapped in handlebar tape, to provide a comfortable grip area and give you more traction than you can get in bare metal. Tape is available in a nearly infinite array of colors and designs and a variety of thicknesses and padding strength. For straight bars it is more common to use slide-on rubber grips for the same purpose.

Always wrap your handlebar tape so the tape travels toward the outside as it goes over the top of the handlebar tube. This allows your hands to tighten the handlebar wrap while they rest in their default position on the bars, making rewrapping less frequent.

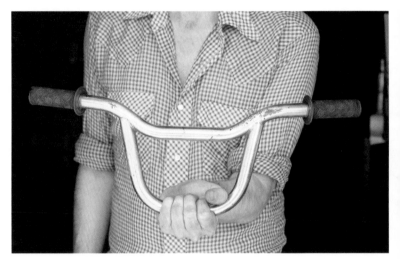

BMX bars

Cruiser bars

HOW-TO:
HACK YOUR BARS

To shorten your handlebars,
you can use a hacksaw.

Attaching a guide helps you keep your
saw cut straight and level.

While it's possible to purchase handlebars in nearly any configuration you want, it's sometimes most efficient to hack them yourself. You may want to shorten your handlebars for a couple of reasons. You can create homemade bull-horns from drop bars or simply shorten your flat bars.

Bull-horns, or flipped-over drop bars with the ends cut off, are popular because they allow a very stretched out riding position, which is aerodynamic for track racing. They have grown popular in street riding primarily because of their association with track racing and the popularity of track and fixie bikes.

You might want to shorten your flat bars in order to make your bike narrower, which can be useful for riding around the city and wiggling your bike in between narrow canyons of gridlocked cars. Mountain bike bars are generally very wide to provide leverage for climbing uphill, and you won't need that leverage in a flat city.

There are two ways to shorten your bars: with a hacksaw or a pipe cutter.

Hacksaw

A hacksaw cuts in only one direction and is good if you don't have a pipe cutter, but it also has the benefit of not leaving a lip behind that needs to be filed out. However, the cut of a hacksaw blade isn't generally as clean as the cut of a pipe cutter.

1. If the blade is installed correctly, it should cut as you push the blade away from you.

2. Lift the blade gently off the surface you are cutting as you pull the blade back for another stroke. This will save you effort and also prevent the blade from going dull as quickly.

Pipe Cutting

Pipe cutters are used by plumbers to cut pipe and are well suited for working on bikes.

1. Tighten the clamp gently on the bars and rotate it around, gouging the metal.

2. Turn the clamp a quarter turn to tighten it slightly, and rotate the cutter around the bar one half turn, then a quarter back to clear the channel.

3. Tighten the clamp again and repeat until the pipe is cut.

Two important notes:

• Back up the cutter a quarter turn for every half turn forward.

• Only tighten the clamp in tiny increments.

Before you know it, you'll have cut through the pipe.

Note: Cutting with a pipe cutter causes a ridge or lip to fold in inside the bar, which can make it difficult if you plan on putting in bar-end shifters or brakes.

You can also hack your handlebars with a pipe cutter.

Don't over-tighten the pipe cutter; they are easy to break.

HOW-TO: CHANGE YOUR DROP BARS FOR FLAT BARS

One of the easiest conversions, or customizations, bike owners make is to replace their drop bar road bike handles with flat mountain-style bars. It is easy to do this at home.

Before you begin, you need to assemble a few parts. In addition to finding a mountain bike bar of appropriate width and fit for your body, there are several other parts you will need to acquire.

The thickness of the mountain bike and road bike handlebar tubes are not the same, so you will need to get a new stem for your bicycle that fits in your headset (most likely 1 inch [2.5 cm] or 1⅛ inches [2.8 cm], threaded or threadless, as discussed in Bearings, on page 104) to hold your handlebars.

In addition, you will need brake and shift levers that attach to your new handlebars, unless your shift levers are mounted on the downtube of your bicycle.

Make sure you get brake and shift levers compatible with your current system. For instance, not all mountain bike levers work with every type of road bike brake. The variable is how much cable is pulled by the lever as opposed to how much is required by the brake. Similar issues come into play with shifters. If you are going from a 7-speed index system on your drop bars, make sure you get 7-speed index shifters of the same brand for your flat bars.

Often you shorten or bend your straight bars for city riding where you are weaving between cars.

The wingspan of mountain bars is wider to give you more leverage while riding off road.

Mountain brake levers won't fit on the larger diameter road bars.

Road bars have a thicker tube diameter than mountain bars, while in this case the mountain bar has thicker tube walls.

1. Remove your handlebar tape. Do this gently enough that your tape won't rip, so you can reuse it.

2. Release the cable tension on your shifters and brakes. You will need to readjust your brakes and shifters when you are finished; see chapters 10 and 11 for information.

3. Loosen the bolt on the top of your stem if you have a quill-type stem (which looks like a large writing quill, with a tapered end and a wedge bolt) OR loose the 2–4 bolts holding your threadless stem onto the bike. WARNING: With threadless headsets, the stem holds the fork onto the bike; if you don't support the front wheel, it might fall to the ground.

4. Pull the handlebars and stem together off your bicycle; if you correctly loosened your cable tension, the brake and shifter cables will come with it, but not your housing.

5. Place your new stem onto the fork. Make sure the stem you acquired fits properly. With threadless stems there are only two common sizes and a third rare size, but with threaded quill stems there are many slightly different common sizes. Tighten your stem bolt securely.

6. Slide your handlebars through the stem open hole and orient them so they are centered in the stem. Tighten the stem bolt securely.

7. Slide on your shift levers and then your brake levers, or your shift/brake combo levers. Rest the bike on the ground and set your brake levers so they stick approximately 45 degrees out from your handlebar, pointing toward the ground. Use your grips as a measuring device to place your brakes as far out from center as possible while leaving room for your grips. Match the angles with your two levers and tighten the lever down.

8. Before placing your grips on the bike, rethread your shifters and brakes and readjust them. It is important to do this before placing your grips on the bike.

9. Slide your grips onto the bike.

MATERIALS AND TOOLS

- Flat bars
- Brake levers (check against your brakes)
- Shifters that fit the flat bar
- Allen wrench
- Hacksaw or pipe cutter
- Grips

A long, thin screwdriver is great for opening up a space to spray soapy water when removing grips, if necessary.

Many riders put a coin in the bottom of their grips to prevent the bar from cutting through the rubber.

REMOVING HANDLEBAR GRIPS

Straight bar grips are held onto the handlebar with friction. During the course of a riding day, they are placed under repeated rotation pressure as you ride and steer, so they are designed to create a firm bond with the handlebar, which makes them difficult to take off and on when customizing your bike.

To remove grips with an air compressor, attach the needle nozzle, lift up on part of the grip, stick the end of the nozzle in, press down on the actuator lever, and the grip should blow right off. With a bit of practice this technique can also be used to expand a grip slightly to slide it onto the handlebar.

If you don't have an air compressor, things get more complicated. Do not use a lubricant to loosen the grips. Lube is designed to never dry, so your grip will never take a firm position on the bar and will always be loose.

Try a bit of soapy water to lubricate the bar. If soap and water isn't enough, a long thin screwdriver, slid under the cuff for leverage, can also help remove the grip. Rubbing alcohol also gets them on and off like a charm, and then evaporates. Hand sanitizer has the same effect.

PADDING

Padding was common on BMX bikes in the 1980s, to protect kids from hurting themselves during impact with a bicycle. Pads are available for your top bar in a wide variety of colors and patterns. Pads are useful not only to protect your tender bits if you slip off your saddle, but also to protect your bike from getting the paint scratched when you lock it up. These have the added bonus of covering any branding or logos on your top tube, which can help protect your bike against theft.

In addition to store-bought pads, hand-knitted pads are increasing in popularity.

HOW-TO:
CITIFY A MOUNTAIN BIKE

Ever since the early 1980s, millions of mountain bikes have been pumped out by bicycle manufacturers to an eager public. Even though there is a new trend for fixies and other road bikes, mountain bikes still make a great purchase, especially if you are budget conscious. Typically, the cheapest mountain bike available new at a bicycle shop costs less than half of the cheapest road bike.

Road tires vs. knobby mountain tires

Remove the quick-release bolt
that comes with most bikes.

Replace it with a normal bolt from a hardware store;
often you can re-use the original quick-release nut.

Tighten the bolt down to hold your seat in place.

However, a factory mountain bike isn't set up well for road riding. Converting a mountain bike for city life takes only a few simple steps.

1. Swap out your knobby tires for something with less tread. Tire knobs create a high amount of rolling resistance. If you aren't going to be deep in dirt or sand in off-road trails on a regular basis, you'll find yourself with a much greater pedaling efficiency with slick tires. See chapter 9 for information on how to select a tire.

2. Swap out the quick-release seatpost bolt for an Allen nut. While this isn't nearly as good as chaining the seat onto your frame, it will help slow down a thief, and it's as simple as unscrewing the quick-release tab and replacing it with an Allen bolt from any hardware store. Just make sure you bring the cuff from your bicycle to match the thread pattern and length.

PAINTING YOUR BIKE

One popular but difficult way to customize your bicycle is to paint it. There are a spectrum of options available for painting your bike, from the grittiest DIY through hiring custom bicycle frame painting specialists, who often cost as much as the price of a new low-end road bike.

Spray paint. The easiest way to paint a bike is to pick up a rattle can of spray paint at the hardware store and paint away, but this is far from ideal. Since your bike likely has a paint job on it already, the spray paint doesn't have a good surface to adhere to and will quickly start flaking off. I don't recommend this unless you are going for a punk-rock aesthetic, in which case, rattle can away.

Detail work. For simple touch-ups or personal decorations, nail polish and model paint, both of which are formulated for adhering to smooth surfaces such as a painted bike frame, are good solutions.

Powder coating. Popular with gearheads of all sorts, powder coating involves running an electromagnetic charge over raw metal, and then putting it in a room with a cloud of oppositely charged paint, which adheres to the frame evenly and durably. With powder coating, your paint job is incredibly professional looking and durable.

HOW-TO: GET YOUR BIKE POWDER COATED

Preparation

1. Fully assemble your bike (if purchasing a bare frame or used bike) and make sure it all works as planned before embarking on a paint job. Nothing is more frustrating that getting a frame powder coated, then realizing that it has issues that prevent it from functioning properly when reassembled, thus wasting your money and effort.

2. Identify a powder coater in your area willing to do bicycles. Bike shops often have powder coaters they recommend, but if your local doesn't have a recommendation, call the powder coaters in your area.

3. Decide how important color is to you. Setup and cleanup for powder coating is a large amount of the work, so if you are willing to be lumped in with another color batch, you can often save yourself a lot of money. Talk to your chosen powder coater to see if this is possible.

4. Strip all parts off your bicycle. If you are new to mechanics, this might seem intimidating. Be sure to place everything you take off your bike together in one box. Label anything you are unfamiliar with. Keep grouped items (like the headset or the bottom bracket) together in zippered plastic bags to ensure the right pieces stay together.

A frame is prepared for a painting

SUGRU

Painting Day

At the powder-coating facility, they will sandblast off your old paint job, then powder coat your bike. Check with your paint shop to see if they will paint handlebars, stems, and other pieces as well. Be careful; items once powder coated change size and might not fit like before.

Reassembly

1. Face your headset and bottom bracket; in other words, scrape the paint off of these surfaces. These areas have delicate items threaded into them, and if the threading surface isn't perfect your bike's alignment can be thrown off. Extra paint from the powder-coating process can get in the way, so you need to face these surfaces for good fit. This is a difficult and potentially destructive step; if you don't feel confident doing it, most bike shops will only charge a small fee for headset and bottom bracket facing.

2. Reassemble your bike, using the parts you removed.

While I'm reluctant to promote any specific brand or product in these pages, there is a material that doesn't have a clear competitor yet and it's so useful I can't skip it. Sugru is a wonderful material created by a group of U.K. industrial designers with the goal of helping people hack things better.

Sugru is a self-adhesive, flexible, waterproof, dishwasher-proof material that cures at room temperature. It feels like modeling clay and it can be formed into any shape in about 30 minutes before it starts to cure. Let it sit for 24 hours, and it cures permanently into shape with a little bit of flexibility built in for longevity. (It is not brittle when dried, like clay.)

It comes in a variety of colors, and you can mix it like paints to create even more color options.

Sugru is great for fixing up things that are falling apart, such as your old favorite pair of bike shoes that might not be waterproof anymore.

It's also fantastic for doing things with your bike that weren't necessarily intended by the manufacturer.

Sugru can be used to make a more comfortable handlebar grip, permanently attach a bike light to your stem, patch your broken pedals, or customize countless other things on your bicycle.

PAINTED AND CUSTOMIZED: AN IDEA GALLERY

A monochromatic look is one part style, one part art installation, one part head turner.

For transporting a lot of goods on a regular basis, consider front and back brackets for carrying substantial loads, such as on this mail delivery bike.

One-of-a-kind spokes that are evocative of cathedral windows rather than bike shops

Best. Tricycle. Ever.

Pretty in pink.

Changing the color of your tires is a simple, striking way to personalize your ride.

CHAPTER 5:
THE CAR-FREE LIFESTYLE

I own a car. That said, depending on your career and obligations, I believe a car-free lifestyle is entirely possible wherever you live.

I just happen to have a day job (filmmaking) in which I have to drive all over the city, frequently with hundreds of pounds of delicate and expensive equipment. Though I dream of someday making movies entirely off a bicycle, it's not realistic for me right now.

However, it is becoming more and more realistic for many people, and whether or not it's possible for you to go entirely car free, once you start riding your bike you'll be shocked to discover how seldom you actually have to drive your car if you don't feel like it.

STARTING SMALL: A CAR-FREE WEEK

Most of us have spent so much time using our car as our major means of transportation that the idea of going without is initially overwhelming. For this reason, I think it's a great idea to start small, with a car-free week. If even that is too much, try just a car-free day or two.

While every experience will be different, there are many basic variables that affect the decision for most people. Is there a good public transit support system to broaden your scope or work as a backup if your bike fails? Do you have a consistent schedule, or are you often required to go to new places on short notice? How predictable is the weather in your area?

Making the decision to travel entirely by cycle for only a short period forces you to realistically think about your other transportation options, without going into a mental paralysis of imagining doing everything for the rest of your life without a car to support you.

What most people discover is that almost everything they want to do is accessible in one way or another via bicycle. The moment to be overcome is the one where you are about to head out the door and you need to make the decision: do I ride my bike or drive my car? While this decision gets easier the more you ride your bike, on chilly days, when you're running a little late, or when you feel like you have a million things to do, it can be a difficult choice for anyone.

CAR-FREE PERKS

Depending on the traffic patterns in your area, it's likely you'll discover you end up arriving places faster by bicycle than by car, especially during rush hour, since you can zip through traffic and never have to look for parking. If picking up the kids from school, instead of waiting in the inevitable traffic jam of parents you can breeze right to the front and pull your child home in a trailer, or if he is old enough, he can ride on his own.

Additionally, you arrive at your destination refreshed, with your blood flowing in your veins and having already gotten your heart pumping, instead of being sedentary.

The flip side, of course, is that you sometimes arrive sweaty, which isn't always appropriate, and you have to navigate traffic from a more vulnerable position than you might in an automobile.

This means I'm carrying less weight as I ride, and have less chance of damaging my delicate electronics.

Planning ahead can also mean combining trips by waiting to run an errand in a certain neighborhood until you have several reasons to head in that direction to make the cycle trip worthwhile.

Finally, geography comes into play. While few have the luxury of choosing precisely where to live or work based on hill formations, I often plan out my day so I'm climbing hills early on, when I'm fresh, and doing more flat-land errands or downhill riding toward the end of the day.

PLANNING YOUR SCHEDULE

The first step in a car-free week is planning ahead. We do this unconsciously with driving all the time (should I take the freeway or surface streets? Where will I park?), and taking a little bit of that time to plan what your week looks like without a car can make the week easier and more enjoyable.

Whenever possible, think of your social time knowing you won't have a car as an option. If planning an after-work get-together with friends, suggest a location on your route home from work.

It helps to become very conscious of what precisely you need to bring with you. For instance, I stopped bringing my laptop home from the office when I switched to full-time cycle commuting; I rarely use it at home and a smart phone can do in a pinch.

Groceries and Other Weekly Errands

Instead of the big grocery store run in which you load up with all the food you need for a week, which is usually too much to carry on a bicycle, consider shopping market style, two or three times during the week, maybe on your way home from work. Swing by the farmers' market in your area on your bike, too.

Eating to Ride

You should plan ahead to have more food on hand, and healthier options, during your car-free week. Riding a bike creates an appetite, and when it's exercising your body seems to crave healthier food.

Fruits make excellent cycling foods because they tend to come with their own wrapper. A simple sandwich is also a great bring along for a bike ride, or some cut-up vegetables.

Hydration

There is no match for the hydration you get from pure, clean water, and when cycling, it's a good idea to drink 20 ounces (0.5 L) or more an hour. Conveniently, most bicycle water bottles contain around 20 ounces, which makes it easy to monitor your water intake.

Simple, packaging-light foods such as raisins or rolls make excellent cycling foods.

DRINKING AND CYCLING

Though a lot of cyclists take it lightly, drinking alcohol and cycling is becoming an increasing problem as more and more people live their daily lives on their bicycles.

In addition to whatever legal ramifications there are in your area (in most places, it's the same as drinking and driving a car), it's also incredibly dangerous.

Your reaction times are significantly slowed by alcohol, making it more likely you will end up in the path of a motor vehicle, which could mean serious harm to you, the motorist, and/or whatever the motorist hits as she swerves to miss you. It's also possible to crash into static objects while impaired.

If you have had too much to drink, walk your bike home, take public transit, or get a ride.

Adjusting Your Wardrobe and Hygiene for Daily Cycling

Although we discussed cycling attire in chapter 3, there are a few more considerations when discussing a car-free lifestyle.

If you are transitioning out of a lifestyle that wasn't particularly active, or one where you were active only in preset times (gym time, game time) but otherwise sedentary, being active throughout the day might take some adjusting to.

- Depending on where you work, it's probably a good idea to bring along a change of clothes with you, so you can peel off a sweaty jersey and put on a work shirt. Many workplaces offer showers, which are necessary all year but can be a lifesaver during the hot summer months as you work up a real sweat on your way to the office.

- Bring along multiple pairs of socks. I keep a spare set in a plastic bag to contain any odor and swap out at some point during the day. As a bonus, changing your socks in the middle of the day feels totally awesome. (You may want to consider bringing multiple items of other clothing that is worn against your skin, too.)

- Keep a spare pair of shoes at the office or so you can ride to work in cycling shoes but don't have to wear them all day. One bike shop where I worked when I was younger had a shoe cubby like a preschool for all the shoes of the employees who rode to work in bike shoes.

- Carrying a basic travel kit of a small towel, soap, and toiletries allows you to take a quick bird bath in a restroom and cool your body down before you enter a professional environment.

Shoes, a laptop padded sleeve, and a rain jacket in the waterproof pouch of this bag get this rider set for the day.

PARKING YOUR BIKE

Bikes should be parked inside. Because of the necessary mechanical simplicity of a bicycle, all of its important parts are exposed to the elements, and though riding in the rain is no big deal (provided you lube your chain afterward), leaving a bike outside in the rain is a bad idea.

Additionally, leaving your bike outside dramatically increases the odds that some or all of it will be stolen. No amount of bicycle security is perfect, and the longer a thief has access to your bike the more likely that he will be able to steal it.

Combine this with predictably locking your bike in the same place outside your job or house, and it is a recipe for disaster. Even if the thief doesn't have the needed tools to swipe it the first time he spots your ride, once he has seen it in the same place over and over, he gets the opportunity to return with the necessary tools to make off with your bicycle.

If your workplace does not provide secure bike parking, ask them whether you can arrange something.

Most schools provide a dedicated bike parking area of some sort, which is generally full of bikes, covered from the weather, and overseen by the security of the school, which is extremely beneficial.

Locking your bike, U lock

If you have an unpredictable schedule, still be conscious of not being too regular with your parking. I teach one night a week, but go out of my way to park in a different location every week, to avoid the sort of consistency that thieves benefit from.

Bike Parking at Home

Home parking can be initially a little daunting, especially if sharing your home with friends or a companion who doesn't understand your bike love. However, there are numerous options on the market, starting with the lowly hardware store hook on through stands and wall-spreaders that allow you to hang your bike up, putting it on prominent display for your friends to admire while also decreasing the floor space it

occupies in your home. If you have limited square footage, getting the bike up off the floor is a great way to save space.

Many apartment complexes have dedicated bike storage areas for parking your bike. These are a mixed bag, depending on the theft level of your area. They are generally secure, but they are also an area that bike thieves know will be chock-full of bikes, and I know many people who have had either their whole bike or many components stolen from their beloved rides in storage rooms. Be skeptical of parking your bike there until you have investigated.

The best bike parking in the home is the one that makes it the most convenient to get your bike out and ready to ride.

HOW-TO:
GO ON A BICYCLE DATE

Depending on your current relationship status, if you start riding your bike frequently, you might end up on a bicycle date. Maybe it's because of how much I love cycling, but I think there are few things quite as romantic as sharing a bike ride and a meal with someone when the weather and the lighting are just right.

1. If loaning your date one of your spare bikes, be sure to take the time to make sure it fits properly and he or she understands every aspect of its function and feels safe and confident on it.

2. Plan a ride that is not incredibly difficult, even if you are both experienced cyclists. Though you can always deviate from the plan and go race each other up steep hills, it's usually a good idea to start slow. A date is hopefully an excuse to get to know each other, and it's hard to chat freely while panting like a dog and pedaling furiously to keep up.

3. Bring layers. Most dates happen in the afternoon or evening, and as the sun sets or the night gets later, it could get chilly. Providing an extra layer for your date, regardless of your respective gender(s), is considered the height of chivalry.

4. Wear a jersey or cycling pants. If you end up riding in front, plumber's crack isn't considered sexy by many.

Of course, not all dates are romantic in nature, and cycling can make a great replacement for other social engagements in life. Instead of a leisurely round of golf, a vigorous bicycle ride can be a great business-networking event, including a good amount of competitiveness along with camaraderie.

TAKING A CYCLING VACATION

You wake up, get on your bicycle, and start riding. You ride all day, through the chilly morning and into the hot afternoon and the cool of evening, knowing that the only thing you are going to do that day is ride your bike. You're going to sleep 50 or 100 miles (80 to 160 km) from where you woke up, and you will have gotten there on your own power. Sleep, then wake up and go again. Sound like fun?

Hammocks are lightweight to carry on a ride and often worth the effort.

If it does (and to me, it kind of sounds like heaven), then a bike vacation might be for you. Generally referred to as bike touring (see more on touring bicycles in chapter 1), traveling by bike can be loosely defined as anything that gets you out on the bike for long periods of time.

There is really no feeling like traveling great distances on your bike under your own power. Because you pedal up every hill and coast down even the smallest downhill, you develop more of a sensitivity to the contours of the earth than you would in a car, or even walking.

Touring on a dedicated bicycle trail.

Both forms of touring have their perks and drawbacks. A quick overnight weekend out of town can be great unsupported; a full week on the road might require more support. Or it might not—friends of mine recently planned a three-week unsupported ride in the American Pacific Northwest, and returned to normal life elated.

One major difference between a road trip in a car and a cycle tour is you realize how much space there is between cities. On a road trip, you might spend a day or two in a town and then drive a few hours to the next, and the places don't seem very far apart. When riding your bike through the countryside, it often takes several days to reach the next major town, which you might pass through in a matter of minutes. Once arriving in an urban area, you discover even the largest cities can be ridden from one end to the other in under an hour, occasionally two, and then you are back to the country again.

TOURING SUPPORT NETWORKS

Touring is divided into two broad camps: supported and unsupported.

Supported touring often refers to organized, multiday charity rides where a support van carries all travel gear for the riders, there are designated water stops, and so on, but it doesn't have to be that systemized. Supported touring can also refer to using the support of modern conveniences, such as motels and credit cards, as you ride from place to place. Supported tourists enjoy the fact that their bikes weigh much less because they have to bring much less with them on board the bike.

Unsupported touring is a multiday ride where you bring everything you need with you, and camp along the way. Fans of unsupported riding enjoy the freedom of riding wherever they like without worrying about finding a motel to sleep in or a restaurant to eat at. Many of them like getting away from modern conveniences.

PLANNING BASICS

Planning is an essential element in any bike trip, whether supported or unsupported.

Weather. Many folks, embarking on their first long bike trip and having spent most of their life in mostly temperature-controlled environments, aren't prepared for what it actually means to be outside all day every day for several days in a row.

- Be sure to consult local weather online for the area where you will be riding.

- If it's too far in advance for online weather tools, an almanac (such as the *Farmer's Almanac*) is an accurate guide to weather up to a year in advance to give you a sense of general trends.

Know the distance. If you are planning a supported ride, make sure that the distance between stops is reasonable, or flexible, if possible.

- Know a good cover location in case weather changes quickly.

- If you don't have it in you to ride 170 miles (275 km) uphill, find a good motel halfway.

- Build in slack time; you might not feel like riding all day every day.

- Even with a supported ride, make sure you will be going past water stops every 20 to 30 miles (30 to 50 km). Most campsites offer some sort of water pump, which is essential.

Gauge terrain. It's a good idea to use satellite-view or topographic maps to get a sense of how hilly or mountainous the terrain might be. If possible, give yourself an easier first day; you'll still be working out kinks in your system and getting your body adapted to the ride.

Crowd sourcing ... or not. A good search of online forums will turn up some good routes, but it's sometimes fun to strike out with just a map and go exploring. If you are using Internet maps, check to see if the roads you are planning to use are private; often what looks like the best roads to ride on a map turn out to be closed to the public or otherwise inaccessible.

Train, train, train. If you haven't ever cycle toured before, a series of training rides can be a great way to gauge how far you like to ride in a day. Experiment with different methods of attaching gear to your bicycle. Your first idea for packing might not be the best. Before our first tour, my buddy and I did "century Sundays" in which we rode 100 miles (160 km) every Sunday for several months to get our bodies prepared for the long riding and get mentally used to spending all day on a bicycle.

WHAT TO PACK

While compiling an exhaustive checklist is possible, your needs will be different for every ride and every rider. Here are a few basics that make any ride go more smoothly. See the chapter on Required Tools for more information.

Packing List: Supported Tour

- Be sure to bring along a small package of frequently used tools:
  - Allen key
  - Spoke wrench
  - Tire levers
  - Patch kit
- **A very long frame pump.** The short frame pumps are great when just filling your tire a little to get to a bike shop; if you need to fill to full pressure to ride on another 70 miles (113 km), a long frame pump is the next best thing to a floor pump.

- **Layers of clothing.** It's likely to be chilly in the morning, even in the height of summer, and daytime can warm up quite a bit no matter the season. Being able to strip off layers as your mood and body temperature change throughout the day will make you more comfortable.

- **Change of clothing.** Everyone remembers his preferred cycling clothing for riding all day, but many riders forget to pack an outfit for those serene hours when you are off the bike. Make it light (jeans are comfortable but heavy). It is unbelievably pleasurable to slip into clean clothes at the end of the ride, rather than the sweaty grubs you've been wearing all day and that you are about to wear the next day.

For men, changing into a thin pair of slacks might make you feel classy and put together.

For women, a light dress, pants, or skirt and top will be a pleasant change from the daily uniform.

- **Water bottles or a backpack bladder.** While riding, you should be drinking at least 20 ounces (0.5 L) of water every hour. If you feel thirsty, you've already waited too long. Sipping frequently is more beneficial than chugging rarely.

- **Reading or writing materials.** Bringing along a book is vital. Even if riding with friends, you'll spend all day chatting; a quick 15 minutes of reading before lights-out can be a great way to get a little quiet time in. Even if you don't usually keep a journal, a notepad is essential. Long rides provide time to chew over thoughts in a way we don't get to in normal life, which can lead to new insights and perspectives.

- **Lighting** for your bike is even more important in the dark countryside than it is in the city. Bring a headlamp for your head as well, since without streetlights it might be impossible to keep riding after sundown, which can be a dilemma if you have a stopping point you need to hit and don't make it by dark.

- **Snacks.** Easily digestible snacks, such as peanut butter sandwiches, granola bars, or fruit are essential.

- **Lightweight raingear.** Just in case. It is worth lugging it with you through several sunny days for that one rainy day.

UNPLUGGING

I do everything I can not to bring a laptop with me when I cycle tour. While a cellular phone can be important for emergency situations, I also prefer not to check it too frequently, if at all possible. No matter how hard I try, electronics always seem to get soaked, with pocket sweat from being too close to my body, or rainwater, or a spill. Even more important, I want to be just on my bike, with my mind on where I am and what's around, and it's hard for me to get there if I know there are work emails to respond to.

Packing List: Unsupported Tour

For an unsupported tour, you'll need all of the above, and more.

- Camping basics, such as a tent, a sleeping pad, and a sleeping bag. You'll also need to bring along enough food to eat without stopping at grocery stores, more water, camping silverware, and bowls and cups.

Consider packing a simple, small lightweight camping stove. Some stoves burn denatured alcohol, which leaves behind less waste than a comparable sterno or tablet system would. Stoves are great for making chili, oatmeal, coffee, or whatever else you want to fuel you on your trip.

CHOOSING A CAMPSITE

Most campsites are built around the car or the backpacker. Thus, most bike-accessible campsites charge fees that provide you enough space to park a large truck or camper, set up a few tents for the family, and get a good cookout going.

Before you commit to staying at a campsite, you may want to consider other issues.

Sharing space with car campers. The culture of car camping is very different from cycle camping. RV campers may stay up late listening to loud music, running generators to keep their lights going, and generally partying. A cycle camper is pretty exhausted by the end of the day and eager to get up early to ride during the nice cool morning hours.

Hobo camping. This camping style is popular with many cycle tourists. Hobo camping is finding any spot where you can peacefully camp for the night. Even if you end up paying to stay at an official campsite to take advantage of their water and shower facilities, you might find yourself hunting for a quiet hobo spot in the woods nearby.

BEGINNING YOUR TOUR

You may want to plan a long ride somewhere not necessarily easy to get to from your home. While the ideal tour starts and ends at your front door, it's not always possible. There are several alternatives, all of which work for one-day or multiweek excursions.

Driving tour. In this tour, you drive to a secure location with the bikes in your truck or on a car rack. You can ride in a giant loop, camping along the way. You could also car camp, driving to a new site every day, and string together a series of day trips.

This has a high level of convenience, but it is not ideal. While a big loop is fun, it isn't nearly as fun as heading out and covering territory and sleeping someplace new—all on your bike.

One-way ticket out of town. Another great option is to take public transit—bus, train, or even plane—then ride home. You don't have to worry about your car being parked somewhere for several days. Also, you are always on the way home—a great motivating force.

BAGGAGE CLAIM

Check ahead of time with your bus, train, or airline and find out about their requirements for bringing your bike along with you. Most are used to arranging for cycle tourists and will have answers for your questions already, possibly on their website. In many cases, you'll discover that bringing your bike, fully loaded for your tour, will be simple and efficient.

PACKING YOUR BICYCLE FOR TRAVEL

If you are traveling with your own bicycle on the trip, chances are you will need to pack it in some sort of container (though some train systems have dedicated bike parking).

Any bike shop should have bike boxes galore; bikes come in boxes from the factory, and most shops give the boxes away for free or for a very small fee. Recycling is a good thing.

How-to: Pack Your Bike

1. Remove the front wheel and pedals.

2. Slide the front wheel over the non-driveside crank, then place the entire assembly into the bicycle box.

3. You'll likely notice that the handlebars won't fit; generally you need to loosen the handlebar stem and remove it from the frame in order to tuck the handlebars in sideways.

4. In certain rare situations you'll need to deflate the tires in order to make it all fit; if you do so, make absolutely sure that you have the right pump with you to refill the tires when you arrive.

Another option is a reusable bike travel luggage. Luggage offers the benefits of less waste, but you will need some way of storing it or bringing it with you on your ride. Also, most of these are expensive and designed for competitive road racers who travel with their high-end road bikes.

A convenient option is the messenger bike carrying bag, which allows you to fit your entire bike on your back. This is ideal for any form of travel. Pack everything you need for your trip into a shoulder bag, then throw the shoulder bag into the larger messenger bike bag. Ride to the airport or train station (on your bike, if you can). Pack the bike in the messenger bike bag, check in, check your bike as luggage, and use your shoulder bag as a carry-on.

Packing Luggage on your Bicycle

Whether you are touring supported or unsupported, chances are you'll need bike accessories for packing more than you need when riding daily around town.

Braze-ons. Dedicated touring bikes and many consumer mountain bikes (which can be converted into great touring bikes with some slick tires; see chapter 4) generally have a variety of threaded braze-ons for connecting front and rear racks. These are elements built into the frame that allow you to easily bolt heavy gear to the frame directly without adapters, and they are a great bonus for a long-distance bike tour.

Handlebar bag. The handlebar bag allows you to keep snacks, a cell phone, maps, and other regular sundries within easy reach. A long, hard ride makes food taste especially delicious, and having that food readily available is a real convenience.

Front and rear panniers. For short trips a single set of panniers is usually enough. Use one pair of panniers, either front or back, with your tent/sleeping bag/bed pad rolled into a pouch strapped on top of them. Panniers often come in pairs because it allows you to split the weight to both sides of your frame, which makes your bike handle more predictably. The bike will pull toward whichever side is weighted when you lean into a turn; it's easier to handle a bike that pulls both ways roughly evenly.

> Any weight on your fork or handlebars, be it a handlebar bag or front panniers, will change the handling of your bike. Do several practice rides before your tour to make sure you can safely operate the bike in those conditions.

Trailer. Some people enjoy touring with a bike trailer instead of loading up their frame.

The benefits of trailers (which are produced by several manufacturers) include:

- They can generally be fitted to any bike regardless of frame braze-ons.
- They can hold a significant chunk of weight.
- They keep the weight low to the ground, which keeps your handling stable.

The drawbacks of a trailer include:

- They can be heavy, which isn't always ideal for long-distance touring.
- They add another point of failure. It's another wheel that could go flat, another connection (between the bike and the trailer) that could get out of whack.
- Drivers might not see a trailer because it is so low to the ground and hit it. For this reason, most trailers come with a flag that sticks up considerably to ensure that it is visible at eye level on the road.

TRAVEL TIPS

Cyclists have been going on road trips (sometimes called randonneuring, or long cycle trips) for more than a century, and there is some accumulated knowledge that is passed down among riders to help make your adventure more enjoyable.

Drafting

Drafting is the technique of using one vehicle traveling through space as a wind shield for a vehicle traveling behind it. Birds do it, drivers looking to save fuel on the freeway do it behind tractor trailers, racecar drivers do it, and cyclists do it. You can learn to do it, too.

The catch: to reap the maximum advantage of drafting, the drafting vehicles need to get pretty close to the other vehicle. Watch any bike race on TV and you'll see riders with their front tire mere inches (centimeters) from the tire of the rider in front of them. If the front person brakes suddenly, the rear rider needs to be alert enough to stop just as quickly, or else she can crash into the front rider and cause an accident.

When touring, the large amount of gear loaded onto each bike slows down the stopping speed of the bicycle and can increase the likelihood of a crash if all riders are not vigilant.

If done with caution, drafting can make a ride, especially one with a headwind, significantly easier.

- Work out a rotation with your cycling group for who takes turns at the front or lead position.

- Only follow as close as you feel safe. When new to drafting, or drafting with an unfamiliar load, it's a good idea to do a few practice stops to see how fast your bike can stop in an emergency.

- If you are one of the followers, don't just watch the tire of the rider in front of you; keep your eyes up and on the road ahead as much as possible to anticipate road hazards that might cause the leader to slow down and slow yourself in anticipation.

- Some riders take turns in the front with a follower who drags the heavy trailer. This leaves the leader taking the brunt of the wind without having the extra trailer weight; if your trailer is easy to switch between riders this can be a great way to ensure variety in your ride.

Health and Hygiene on the Road

This is a delicate subject. On a cycling vacation, you will be sitting on your butt—literally—for 8 to 10 hours a day for a week, generating a lot of sweat, and also friction as you pedal constantly throughout the day. It is extra essential to maintain good hygiene in your nether regions throughout the trip for maximum health and comfort.

- Be sure to be extra thorough in cleaning yourself after going to the bathroom.

- Consider carrying prepackaged wipes or rubbing alcohol and pads for quick, antiseptic swipes over the buttocks and groin area. This will help prevent pores from becoming infected. The alternative is bacteria sticking around and causing a saddle sore, which you don't want if you have another 300 miles (480 km) to pedal to get home.

URBAN LEGEND: DAY 2 & ROAD GRUMPINESS

For some reason, day 2 of any long bike trip seems like the worst day of the trip. It's the day our bodies realize they're going to keep riding, day after day, without a break. Our legs feel like they have lead in them. Every hill seems like a reason to take a break. Everything our riding companions say sounds like an insult. This is road grumpiness.

This too shall pass. The most important thing to remember is that it will pass, and that it's nothing personal. Keep riding, slowing the pace for the day if you have to. Maybe eat some healthy sugar, like a banana. If you are riding in a larger group and the dynamics get really tense, spread out the riding pack so everyone isn't right on top of each other.

Lightening the load. Day 2 is often a good time to find a post office and send a package home. After the first day and night on the road, you will discover that 25 percent of your gear is unnecessary. Boxing it up and sending it home can give you a great, lightweight feeling for the rest of your ride. Knowing that you aren't dragging around those extra jeans or a copy of *War and Peace* will get you great mental mileage.

Hard to believe, but on the inside he's ready to explode with grumpiness.

PART II: THE BICYCLE

CHAPTER 6:
BICYCLE ANATOMY

Your bicycle can be broken down into a few main parts: the frame, the drive train, the braking system, and the steering system. Understanding the function and purpose of all the basic elements of a bicycle is essential to being able to repair and customize your bike.

BASIC MECHANICS

There are a few basic mechanical concepts that should be covered before you dive deeply into repairing your bicycle.

FRAME

The double-triangle frame that most of us are accustomed to is known as the "safety frame."

It was introduced in the late nineteenth century as a safer alternative to the penny farthing, which consisted of the huge front wheel/tiny rear wheel that has become an iconic Victorian-era symbol. (You still see these bikes ridden ironically around town by a dude with a mustache from time to time.)

The basic components of a safety frame are:

1. Top tube, which runs along the top of the bike

2. Head tube, the small tube at the front of the frame and contains the headset, the bearing assembly that allows the fork to turn

3. Downtube, which runs at an angle from the head tube to the bottom bracket

4. Bottom bracket shell, which holds the bottom bracket, the area at the bottom of the frame that holds the bearing assembly that allows the cranks to turn

5. Seat tube, which runs from the bottom bracket up toward the seat

6. Seat stays, which run from the top tube/seat tube cluster to the rear dropouts

7. Chainstays, which run from the bottom bracket to the rear dropouts

8. Dropouts, which is where the wheel mounts to the frame; two sets, front and rear

9. Fork, which holds the front wheel in place and connects to the handlebars

While there are many variations on this basic design, this is the basic layout of a bicycle. (See Geometry on page 122.)

KNOW YOUR BIKE

1: top tube
2: head tube
3: downtube
4: bottom bracket shell
5: seat tube
6: seat stays
7: chainstays
8: dropouts
9: fork

THREAD AND THREAD DIRECTION

Threads are one of the essential elements of modern fasteners. They are the angled grooves on a threaded rod that pull a nut one way or the other as you rotate the rod, or that pull a screw into what it's screwing.

Crank bolt with grease

Most threaded objects are right-hand threaded, which means if you rotate a nut or thread so the top of the nut is moving to your right, the threaded object will tighten. This leads to the mnemonic phrase, "righty-tighty, lefty-loosey."

However, there are certain places in a bicycle (mostly around the drive train) where left-hand thread is necessary. If you are struggling to free a threaded part of the drive train, check whether the part has left- or right-hand thread. It's possible to strip the fastener quite badly while trying to loosen it if you twist it the wrong way.

GREASING THREADS

Every threaded surface on a bicycle should be coated with a little dab of grease before it is threaded.

While this might seem counterintuitive (usually we grease things in life to help them move freely or slip off), it does four important things.

1. It allows you to get the nut or bolt tighter than you would otherwise, which engages the spring force of the metal to secure it.

2. It fills in all the microscopic gaps in any threaded system, making the connection less likely to loosen because of vibrations.

3. It prevents metal-to-metal bonding. Any two like metals, when pressed together for long enough, will bond together to form a single piece of metal. To prevent this, it's also important to grease seatposts and handlebar stems to prevent them from permanently seizing.

4. While most materials on a modern bicycle (aluminum, titanium, and stainless steel) don't oxidize, a grease coating can protect any steel parts on your ride from oxidizing, otherwise known as rusting.

CABLE ACTUATION

Most braking and shifting systems on a bicycle use a system of cable actuation to translate input from the handlebars to systems throughout the bike. In layman's terms, cables are used to transmit the force of your braking or shifting from the handlebars (where your hands rest) to the brakes or derailleurs (where the force is needed).

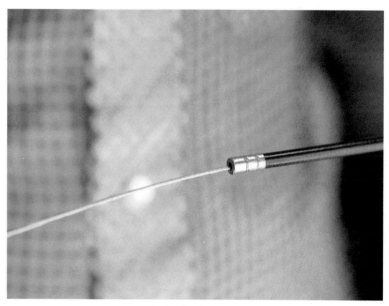

Brake cable with housing

When you move a lever (brake or shift), it pulls or pushes a length of cable through the housing, which is the cover for the cable that runs along with it. At the other end of the housing, the same amount of cable gets pushed in or out, directly applying the lever force to whatever needs it, be it shifter or brake.

As you work on your bike, and especially once you start modifying it, understanding the concept that allows cables to work is vital. As you push or pull the cable at one end, a corresponding and equal amount of cable pushes or pulls out the other end of the housing, which allows you to move lever force around the bicycle wherever you need it. The difference in the length of the cable and housing is what transmits the force.

BEARINGS

Bearings make most of the things in the world that go round go round, including car wheels, the turbines in power generators, and the propellers in airplanes. The most common type of bearing on a bicycle is the ball bearings, which are tiny spherical metal balls that come in a wide variety of sizes. The bearings hold the axle (which is the rotating element) in place and allow it to spin freely.

Your bicycle has several items that need to rotate: the wheels rotate around their hubs, the cranks rotate around the bottom bracket, the pedals rotate on their axis, and the handlebars twist back and forth around their headset.

A ball-bearing set consists of a cup, a cone, and the balls. The bearings (or balls) sit in the cup, which is attached to part of the spinning assembly, and the cone sits on the bearings. With ample grease applied to the system, the cone and cup can spin against each other with very little wear on the system. This allows your wheel to spin while the axle that bolts to your frame stays static, and allows your cranks to spin while your bottom bracket stays in place.

Bearings on a bicycle are usually available in adjustable or sealed styles. Adjustable styles are more common, and offer the benefit of weighing slightly less and of being repairable, so as they age they can be maintained. Sealed bearings are popular because they are weatherproof, but when they wear out, they need to be entirely replaced. Well-made sealed bearings can last a decade or more.

As you modify your bike, or simply maintain it over the years, you will need to understand how to adjust or repack your bearings. See How-to: Repack Loose Ball Bearings on page 145.

Cutaway view of head tube and headset assembly

THE LOCKNUT

A locknut twists two nuts together on a threaded rod, which fixes their positions (preferably not flush against the bearings).

Adjustable bearing systems are dependent on locknuts. Usually, in order to tighten a bolt or nut, you simply tighten as far as you can. With a bearing system, tightening a bolt completely locks the cone against the balls, which causes the bearings to freeze. The cone should be left adjusted so that the cone rests gently against the bearings without applying pressure on them. Further instructions on adjustable bearing adjustment are in chapter 10.

Bearing cages

WRENCHES

For a discussion of why you should not use an adjustable wrench for fixing bicycles, please see page 56.

A good wrench set, with a box end on one side and an open wrench on the other, is the best tool to use when working with nuts. Because of the amount of contact surface between the wrench and the nut, it is almost impossible to strip a nut when using a box-end wrench.

DRIVE TRAIN

The drive train of a bicycle is the system of pedals, cranks, chainrings, chain, derailleur, shifters, cogs, and wheels that allow the rider to propel herself forward.

Gears are what allow the bike to be easier to pedal when going uphill and then harder to pedal downhill, which lets you go faster. The larger the gear is in front next to the pedals, the harder it is to pedal. It may be counterintuitive, because it's not the same for the gears attached to your pedals, but the larger the gear attached to your rear wheel, the harder it is to pedal. Typically in front you have two or three widely spaced gears that cover a broad range: the little "granny gear" for climbing large hills, your middle gear for flat land, and your big ring for downhill. The rear gears are more closely spaced together for finer changes in the pedaling force.

The larger a gear, the more teeth it has to engage the chain. Your front gears will likely have a range, such as 34/42/50 teeth (for a road bike) or 26/36/44 teeth (for a mountain bike), while your rear gears will be divide in one- or two-tooth increments (a 7-speed cluster might only cover a range of 12 to 28 teeth).

The merging of gearing and pedal power in cycling is one of the greatest revolutions in the history of mechanics. Before gearing, people rode around on penny farthings, which had enormous front wheels because the direct connection between the pedals and wheels required a huge wheel to get anywhere. This principle applies to "big wheel" children's bikes, too: a bigger wheel lets you go faster when your pedals are attached to your wheel.

Most shifter systems control the drive train through cable actuation (please see page 103). A long steel cable runs from the shifter lever (where you manually change gears) to the derailleur, through housing. The most important thing to understand is that it's the difference in the length of the cable and the housing that is important. The housing does more than just protect against the weather; it also has a structural function in shifting. As you move the cable in and out of one end of the housing, the cable at the other end moves in and out the same amount, and that force adjusts your derailleur. This means it is important to run the housing consistently along the entire length of the cable, since it plays a structural part in the cabling system.

DRIVE TRAIN VARIATIONS

The main variations in drive trains are how many gears you have and how those gears are shifted. Most bikes with multiple speeds shift gears using derailleurs, which physically force the chain to shift between chainrings (in front) and cogs (in back) of various sizes to adjust the intensity of your pedaling.

Internal gear hubs hide the gearing inside an oversized rear hub, most commonly associated with the classic English 3-speed. Originally, the hubs contained two or three widely spaced gears; they now frequently contain up to 7 or 14 speeds.

Unfairly associated with slow bikes because they are slightly heavier than a comparable derailleur system, internally geared wheels make a lot of sense in certain circumstances. They offer several benefits:

- They always have a perfectly straight chain, which noticeably increases pedaling efficiency.

- They offer much higher weather-proofing than is possible with a derailleur system because the gears are packed away inside a hub.

If you are a rider in an area with a lot of rain or snow, an internally geared hub might make sense. The old-school range (3-speed) has gone out of fashion and 6–7 speeds are more typical on a modern bike, which provides plenty of range for even a hilly city.

While there are 14-speed internally geared hubs on the market, they are targeted primarily at racers and are very expensive.

GEAR RANGE VS. SPEEDS

The number of "speeds" a bicycle has refers to the number of options you have for different gear ratios. The classic road bike of the 1970s had 10 speeds: two gears in front (but no granny gear for hill climbing) and five in back. By going to three speeds in front, and putting more gears across the rear cluster to get up to 7 speeds, 21 speeds quickly became the norm by the 1990s. Seeing as many as 10 speeds across the rear cluster (leading to a 30-speed bike) is now common.

However, even in 10-speed, there are redundant gears; for instance, with certain bicycle setups a 50 x 19 (50-tooth big chainring, combined with the 19-tooth rear cog) is nearly identical in force to a 42 x 16 combination. So, even a 10-speed isn't really a 10-speed, because there are redundant combinations of gears. Even though you get "21 speeds" with 7 in the back and 3 in the front, there is actually a smaller number of different "gears."

A 21-speed bike also doesn't necessarily have a wider gear range than an 18- or a 15-speed bike. It might have the same top and bottom gear and only have finer gradations along the way.

Fine gradations in the gear range are useful for racers; racing cyclists train to be at maximum efficiency at a very specific cadence (which is the rate of pedal rotations per minute). Having very fine gradations between the rear gears allows racers to stay at their peak cadence regardless of fine changes in terrain.

Gears became a popular way of discussing bicycles because it is an easy-to-use term in marketing; it's very easy to sell 21-speeds as superior to 18-speeds because 21 is a larger number, even if it doesn't offer any real benefits to the average rider.

BRAKING

MEASURING YOUR GEAR

There are several methods currently in use to measure the mechanical advantage that can be gained in the variety of gear combinations. It is not as simple as comparing the number of gears in use in each bike because the size of the wheel affects the comparison.

The most common method in use is gear inches, which compares the gear ratio to the diameter of the wheel. For instance, 85 gear inches would mean riding a bike with an 85-inch-diameter wheel. However, gear inches don't take into account the length of the cranks, which also affects how difficult it feels to pedal your bike.

A simpler, but less common, system is gain ratio. This takes the distance the bicycle moves forward in space and divides it by the circumference the pedals travel.

There are a variety of gain-ratio and gear-inch calculators available online to help you calculate your own measurements. My favorite is Sheldon Brown's at sheldonbrown.com/gears.

In order to be safe, a bicycle must stop. The braking system of your bicycle is designed to bring your bike to a stop quickly and efficiently. Any good bicycle should have at bare minimum two brakes; on most bikes, this is the front and back brakes, but it could also be a coaster brake/fixie and a rim brake combo.

Top: brake cable; bottom: shifter cable

The most common form of brakes are rim brakes, in which the friction of a brake pad against the wheel's rim slows the spinning wheel. Increasingly popular on mountain bikes are disc brakes, in which pads are pushed in against a metal disc that is bolted to the hub. Disc brakes offer faster stopping and better performance in a variety of weather conditions, but tend to be slightly heavier and more expensive than rim brake systems.

With the exception of hydraulic disc brake systems, most brakes are cable actuated, similar to shifters, and attached to levers on your handlebar. However, the brake housing is slightly different from shifter housing in that it is designed to squish slightly, building a little bit of flex into the system to make your braking less abrupt.

Fixed-gear bikes, discussed in detail in chapter 12, can also be considered as having a braking system because you can slow pedaling to stop. Long associated with lower-end bicycles and cruisers, coaster brakes are coming back into style. Coaster brakes, in which you brake by pedaling backward, are popular because of their simplicity of design.

Caliper brakes

To satisfy legal requirements in most areas, not to mention also good common sense, there should be two braking systems on the bicycle, so you have a backup in case one of your braking systems fails. Most bikes accomplish this with two rim brakes, one attached to the front wheel and one attached to the rear wheel.

The brake works by a lever attached to the handlebars to pull a cable that then uses levers mounted by the wheel to push brake pads. The force of the stiff rubber brake pads pushing into the rim slows the wheel.

CALIPER

Road bikes typically use a caliper-style braking system, which encircles the wheel and clamps down on it. They are relatively lightweight and require very simple mounting on the frame (one bolt hole). However, they rarely have enough clearance for a fender, and they aren't as powerful as their counterpart, the cantilever option described below.

They fall broadly into a few types, side pull vs. center pull, and single pivot vs. dual pivot.

Cantilever brakes

Pros: Great stopping force and fender clearance

Cons: Heavier, frames need to be built for them

DISC

For mountain biking, disc brakes are becoming more and more common. Instead of using pads that clamp down on the rim, pads clamp down on a metal disc bolted to the hub, either hydraulically or mechanically. Disc brake systems offer great braking power, especially in wet conditions, which might slow braking on a rim brake. However, they weigh more than a rim brake system.

Pros: Stopping power, especially in wet weather

Cons: Weight, price

Side-pull brakes, more common on newer bikes, have brake housing that go all the way to the brake lever. Old bikes more commonly used center-pull brakes, which required a built-in housing stop (see photo) to provide cable tension. If you want to use center-pull brakes on a more modern bike, stop adapters, which provide the stops you need, are available.

Pros: Lightweight

Cons: Weaker than other designs, sometimes lack room for fenders

CANTILEVER

Cantilever brakes are more common on mountain bikes, but are also found on touring bikes because of their fender clearance and great stopping power. They also include a new derivative design known as the V-brake. These brakes use two levers with the pads mounted above the pivot points; the cable is used to pull the tops of the levers together, applying a strong braking force to the rims. Drawbacks of this system are that it requires more complicated mounting on the frame (two pivot posts) and weighs slightly more, though for most applications the trade-offs are worth it.

COASTER

Coaster brakes are enjoying a renaissance, but are most commonly found on cruisers and kids' bikes. A coaster brake is a drum brake, in which brake pads push out on a barrel from the inside. On a bicycle, the barrel is the inside of the rear hub, with pads inside that push out and apply braking force when you pedal backward. Mechanically very simple and durable, they are fantastic for a bike that will be used for running errands in the neighborhood.

Pros: Retro-cool

Cons: Somewhat weak

HOW-TO:
ADJUST YOUR BRAKES

If you have to press the brake lever all the way to the handlebar to stop, your brakes might be too loose and require adjustment. Properly adjusted brakes feel firm to the grip and stop the bike quickly while you are riding.

Using a brake alignment tool on center pull brakes

Before adjusting your brakes, be confident you have the time to finish the job properly before you need to ride your bike anywhere. In order to adjust them, you will need to release their tension, leaving you without brakes.

It's helpful to hang your bike, preferably from a bike repair stand, before you begin to adjust the brakes.

1. Check your brake pad alignment. Your brake pads should hit directly on the rim, straight on when viewed from the side. When viewed from the top, the front of your pad should hit slightly before the rear of your pad to prevent squeaking. This is called "toeing in." If they are not aligned, loosen the nut holding the brake pad in place and adjust the brake pad placement with your fingers, then tighten the nut snugly.

2. Spin your wheel, and slowly tighten your brake cable barrel adjuster until the brake pads start to hit the rim. Then, slowly back out on the barrel adjuster so the pads just barely clear the rim.

3. If your barrel adjuster doesn't give you enough tension for you to be able to stop the wheel spinning by grabbing the brake lever, twist the barrel all the way back in, then out two turns.

4. Loosen the cable tension bolt.

5. Hold the brake pads against the rim.

6. Pull the cable tight and tighten the bolt.

7. Release the pads and adjust the barrel adjuster so that the pads skim just off the rim without rubbing.

8. Test ride in a safe area to get used to your new brake setting.

After you work on your brakes, take a moment for a quick "brake check" before you ride it again. The check is as simple as grabbing hold of the brakes while the bike is on the ground and pushing the bike forward and backward. The wheels should lock up firmly and the bike should resist being pushed. Once you release the brakes, the wheels should then spin freely.

HOW-TO:
GET RID OF BRAKE SQUEAK

Brake squeak is the curse of older and weathered bicycles, but can generally be fixed with a few simple techniques. While the squealing noise is very unpleasant, it is also an indicator that your braking system is aging and needs adjustment.

1. Look at your brakes from above: do the pads hit the rim all at the same time? If so, toe them in by adjusting them so the front of the pad hits slightly before the back. On a modern brake this is easily done once you loosen the pad mounting. With older brakes you will need to twist the arm of the brake caliper.

2. Remove the brake pads and inspect them: is the surface shiny? If so, metal shavings from the rim have embedded themselves in the rubber of the pad. Take some sandpaper and rough up the surface of the brake pad.

3. If you still have squeak, the rubber in your pads might've hardened. Try replacing them with new pads.

STEERING

The steering system of your bicycle consists of handlebars (which are also used to mount the shifters and brake levers); a stem that connects the bars to the fork; a headset, which contains the bearings that allow the fork to spin in the frame; and the fork.

Above about 5 mph (8 km/hour; a gentle roll) most riders don't tend to turn their handlebars more than about 5 degrees. When the rider is at speed, most steering is achieved through a combination of very gentle steering and leaning the bicycle. With practice and a dry road surface, experienced cyclists can lean into a turn and maintain a very high speed through a turn.

See Customization for more about various styles of handlebars.

Threaded and threadless steerer tubes

Fork

Headset

One of the longest-lasting myths of cycle fit is stand-over height: stand over a frame and hold the bike upright. If you have an inch (2.5 cm) of room on a road bike or 3" to 4" (7.6 to 10 cm) on a mountain bike, that is your frame size of choice.

While this is a great place to start with sizing, and was adopted by many bike shops because it's so easy to demonstrate, it is by no means definitive.

I can't stand over any of my bikes except my mountain bike, and there I only have an inch (2.5 cm) or so of clearance, and yet all of my bikes fit me. I like a large frame, because it raises the top bar and also the headset, which makes for higher handlebars and a higher sitting position; I find this more comfortable and it keeps my head up and looking around at the scenery, which is one of the reasons I ride a bike in the first place.

Q-FACTOR

The mysterious-sounding Q-factor, named by Grant Peterson in the early 1990s, is the distance between your pedals. The Q-factor affects your pedaling efficiency. To find the Q-factor, line up your cranks and measure the distance between the outside of each crank.

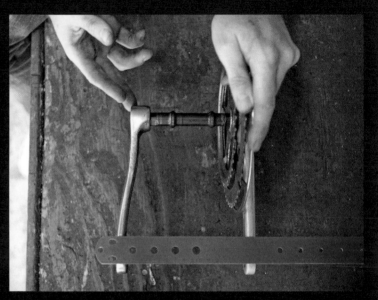

Measuring the distance between crank arms

Most low-end bikes are designed with what are nicknamed birthing cranks: very wide cranks that are designed to clear the chainstays of any frame they are put on, no matter how wide the frame or what bottom bracket is used.

Unfortunately, when your legs are splayed out too far while pedaling you aren't pedaling as efficiently as you would be if the pedals were directly underneath your hips.

To achieve the lowest possible Q-factor, giving you greater pedaling efficiency, use the shortest bottom bracket and narrowest cranks possible without hitting your frame. The frame needs to be wide enough to clear your rear tire. Most cyclists find themselves most comfortable on a bike that allows their legs to move straight up and down. (See chapter 10 for more on bottom brackets and cranks.)

SIZING

It's important to find a bicycle that fits your body type; riding a bike that is too small will leave you cramped and uncomfortable, while riding a bike that is too large will leave you feeling perched and unsafe.

A bicycle is designed with a number of adjustments to fit a wide range of body types. Your saddle can be raised or lowered on its seatpost, your handlebars can be raised or lowered on the stem, and a longer or shorter stem can be used. Bicycle frames are sold in small size increments (2 centimeters for road bikes and 2 inches for mountain). If you find the perfect frame for you but it's a few centimeters off, you can usually adjust other components to accommodate your body.

The most common way to measure size is from the center of the bottom bracket along the seat tube up to the center of the top tube (this is known as center-to-center or c-c). Some brands measure c-t, or center of the bottom bracket to top of the top tube, along the seat tube. Once you

find the size frame you like to ride, knowing how frames are measured can help you pick out other frames that will fit.

However, many would argue that top tube length is even more important than seat tube length in deciding on your bike frame, because it's so easy to adjust frame height (move your seat up or down), whereas you need to swap out your stem to adjust for frame length.

THE IMPORTANCE OF FRAME LENGTH

Frame length dictates how you sit on a bike, which has a huge effect on comfort. A long top tube stretches you forward, whereas a short top tube bends you over the bike at a steep angle. You may like a slightly longer top tube if you have long arms. Ultimately, you should choose a frame with your own personal comfort in mind.

Smaller frames are more popular with racers for a few reasons:

- They force you to bend over more, which makes you more aerodynamic.
- The frames are slightly lighter, which is a priority for racers.

However, racing sizing can be uncomfortable for the average bicycle commuter and others who don't sacrifice comfort for speed.

With a larger frame, you can have stand-over height if you have a low bottom bracket. Bottom bracket height is measured in drop, which is how far below the bottom bracket is from an imaginary line drawn between the two hubs. When there is a large bottom bracket drop, a bike's center of gravity gets very low to the ground. Many riders enjoy a low center of gravity because of how easy it is to lean through a turn.

Mountain bikes and cyclocross frames tend to have higher bottom brackets so they can have more clearance over obstacles.

The most important aspect of fit is that you are comfortable on your bike, and that might change day to day. Be prepared to tweak your saddle height often, and to let your bike grow with you. You might discover after a few months of riding that you are more flexible and want to move your handlebars somewhere that would've been uncomfortable a few weeks earlier.

While comfort varies from person to person, there are a few things you should look out for. Knee pain, especially during riding, is a bad thing, and can be alleviated by tweaking your saddle height. Also be sure to look out for any numbness in your crotch, back, arms, or hands; numbness can be prevented by adjustments to seat height and angle, and handlebar height.

CHAPTER 7: FRAMES

A cult object to some, an afterthought to others, the bicycle frame is what holds your bike together and is considered to be the soul of the bicycle.

If you took all the parts off your frame and built the same frame up with brand-new parts, most of your friends probably wouldn't notice (unless your friends are bike geeks). But if you took all your parts and swapped out your frame, everybody would notice,

How a frame is made and what it is made off radically affect how a bike feels, but never be afraid to let appearance affect your decision as well. We ride bikes we like more than we ride bikes we don't like, and if you like a pretty bike more, there is nothing wrong with that.

FRAME MATERIALS

There are two common frame materials (steel and aluminum) along with a variety of special-use materials (carbon fiber, titanium, bamboo) for making bicycle frames.

Aluminum frame

Steel frame

"STEEL IS REAL"

Until the 1980s or so, the majority of bicycles, from the cheapest mass-market bicycles to the highest end Tour de France–winning racing bikes, were made of steel.

The most common alloy used in bicycles is chromoly steel (for the chromium and molybdenum content of the steel), though there are some obscure bikes that are made of different alloys.

Steel makes a fantastic frame material because it has some flexibility built in, which means that small bumps and road vibrations are eaten by the frame and don't make it all the way up to the rider.

The other benefit steel offers is its malleability. If you bend an aluminum frame (which is hard to do, but possible), the frame is done; it can't be bent back without breaking. But if you bend a steel frame, it can be bent back into place without compromising the frame. Additionally, small adjustments in the frame (like changing the width of the rear dropouts to accommodate a new hub) can easily be accomplished with steel, but is impossible with aluminum.

Pros: Inexpensive, malleable, dampens road vibration

Cons: Heavy if made cheaply, some flex in drive train

ALUMINUM

The other common frame material is aluminum, which became a popular material in the 1980s and now dominates the market. Aluminum is capable of being made into much wider tubes; a bicycle with a large bore tube frame is likely to be made out of aluminum.

Aluminum is a very stiff metal, with very little inherent flexibility. This offers some benefit in the drive train (there is no flex when you pedal, so all of your pedaling power goes directly from the pedals to the rear wheel, making it an excellent choice for a racing bike). But that stiffness also translates into a large amount of road vibration for the operator.

When aluminum frames first became popular, it was a good idea to have a steel front fork to soak up road vibration, and to ride slightly thicker tires than you might on a road bike. Some of these features are noticeable on aluminum touring bikes to this day. As aluminum construction has gotten more sophisticated, varying tube wall thickness and shape has been used to maintain drive train stiffness while making for a more forgiving ride.

Pros: Light and cheap, stiff drive train, tube diameter variety

Cons: High road vibration, minor damage can ruin a frame

TITANIUM

Titanium has been used in small parts on bicycles for most of the last century, but became popular in the 1980s as manufacturing moved away from lugged and toward welding (see page 120 for further information). It is in between aluminum and steel in ride feel (stiff, but not too stiff), and those that can afford it consider it one of the best materials.

Pros: Good balance of stiffness vs. dampening

Cons: Expensive

CARBON FIBER

Carbon fiber became common in sporting equipment in the 1970s, after being developed as an advanced aerospace material in the 1960s. Carbon fiber is valued for its lightness and controllable flexibility. For instance, in a bicycle frame, the carbon fibers can be arranged so the frame has a high degree of lateral stiffness (bottom bracket is stiff side to side) while also having a lot of vertical flex (road vibration and impact can be dampened by the frame). It also can be tuned exactly how the bicycle designer wants it.

However, carbon fiber has a major drawback, called catastrophic failure. As most materials reach failure, they show visible signs, most commonly cracking around their failure point. Carbon fiber, however, will often fail without any visible indicator appearing before failure. Because of this phenomenon, carbon fiber parts on commercial airplanes are regularly x-rayed to inspect for the internal damage that might lead to such failure.

For this reason, carbon fiber isn't necessarily the best city bike or daily rider. In order to make a bicycle frame as light as possible (which is one of the goals in making a carbon fiber bike), they tend to not be as durable, and a catastrophic failure of a part like the fork while riding can be extraordinarily dangerous.

Pros: Can control stiffness directionally, very lightweight

Cons: Expensive, can fail catastrophically

BAMBOO

Bamboo is increasing in popularity as a bicycle frame. It offers great vibrational damping combined with good stiffness, and some benefits in terms of being a sustainable material (it's grown, not mined). Usually coated in polyurethane, bamboo isn't perfectly environmentally friendly, and its long-term durability isn't yet known.

Some argue that long-term durability is the wrong goal, that it's better to have a bike you ride a decade, then compost, than a bike you need to melt down to recycle.

Pros: Vibrational damping and stiffness, cost

Cons: Long-term durability unknown

STRUCTURAL FLAWS

The bicycle cooperative where I volunteer is exceptionally careful about carbon fiber donations; if any surface imperfection can be found that appears to weaken the carbon structure, we destroy the carbon fiber component rather than pass it on to a future rider who might be injured by a failure.

This destruction is a fun and educational process. If you take a hammer to something steel or aluminum, each hit has an effect, slowly deforming the piece until it finally rips apart. Not so with carbon fiber. After the first several strikes, the piece holds its form, looking perfect and undamaged. Then, finally, the death blow comes and the piece explodes into bits. Better that it happens on the floor of our shop than on the road.

FRAME CONSTRUCTION

Up until the 1980s, lugged frames were considered the top of the line. Lugs are metal cuffs that the tubes of the frame are inserted into and then brazed in place. Brazing is a low-heat adhesive process that doesn't affect tube integrity and can be thought of as a metal glue.

Lugged frame

Welded frame

LUGGED

While the lugs themselves add some weight to the frame, the tubes can be made thin because they don't need to be strong enough to be welded.

A lugged steel frame provides a very forgiving ride. The steel has vibrational damping, and the lugs also eat up road vibration and small bumps, because the tubes have a little bit of flex to move around within the lug due to the softness of the brazing material. Brazing doesn't get as hot as welding does. If only a small section of the frame is damaged, tube replacement is easier.

Pros and **cons** include:

- Tubes can be replaced
- Heavy due to lug weight
- Classic look

There are many who still prefer a lugged steel frame, whether for beauty, durability, or ride quality. After a brief period when there were only one or two manufacturers continuing to make lugged steel frames (in addition to one-builder custom shops around the country), lugged steel frames are seeing something of a resurgence in the marketplace.

Frame builders use lugs as an area to express individuality and differentiate themselves in the marketplace. Lugs were often hand-worked to customize the design.

WELDED

Welding was long the primary form of manufacture for cheaper frames, since the process was less labor intensive. To withstand the heat of welding, which melts tubes into each other in order to join them, the tubes had to be thick.

However, advances in both tube technology and welding techniques led to very lightweight durable frames being constructed by welding in the 1980s. Cyclists started to use welded steel, then welded aluminum, and finally titanium and carbon fiber bikes (though carbon fiber is not welded but glued).

Pros and **cons** include:

- Tubes destroyed by welding process
- Light, lacking lugs
- Modern look

BUTTING

When shopping for a bicycle or a frame, butting is a good item to hunt for, because it makes the bike lighter and is a good indicator of the overall quality of a bike.

Butting means that the tube wall thickness is varied throughout the tube to create a lighter tube. The tube only really needs to have a thick wall toward the joins; in the middle of the tube, only a thin wall is required.

If you see a frame that is "butted" or "double butted" or the rare "triple butted," this means that the tube wall goes through a variety of thicknesses (three, for triple butted), being very thin in the middle. These frames are more expensive, but lighter weight.

If the frame stickers are gone, you can hear butting in the frame by flicking the tube at various places with your fingernail; the thinner the tube, the higher and "thinner" the sound of the tube as it rings.

GEOMETRY

Although geometry is very use dependent (see the discussion of bottom bracket drop when discussing sizing, page 115), there are a few aspects that are consistent across many geometries.

Seat tube angle is measured against the ground; a 90-degree seat tube would be completely vertical. The greater the seat tube angle, the closer it is to vertical, and the more it is considered to be an "aggressive" geometry. This is because a more vertical seat tube moves the rider farther forward over the pedals, which allows for great power in the downstroke, but is less comfortable.

As the seat tube angle gets smaller, the rider gets slightly more comfortable at the expense of a small amount of power. Larger frames of the same type tend to have more relaxed seat tube angles; for instance, a 53-cm racing bike might have a seat tube angle of 75 degrees, while a 62-cm frame might have an angle of 74 degrees, and the same ride characteristics.

The same is true of head tube angle; steeper is more aggressive, and more relaxed is more comfortable.

If you are looking for a more comfortable ride, look for a more relaxed seat tube and head tube angle. If you are interested in an aggressive racing bike that gives you the most speed possible, more angles that are bigger are a good choice.

Another factor affecting comfort in geometry is chainstay length. Longer chainstays are more stable; shorter chainstays, more nimble. For city riding, I have always ridden a short chainstay bike to weave more easily through traffic, but if you are carrying a lot of weight, especially on the back of your bike, longer chainstays can be a better option.

SUSPENSION

People have experimented with bicycle suspension since at least the 1880s. Bianchi began mass-producing bikes with suspension for the Italian army during World War I. At its simplest, suspension absorbs the impact of the bicycle against obstacles, which makes a smoother ride for the cyclist. Modern suspension is made up of spring or air shocks, either built into the fork (front suspension) or built into the rear triangle of the frame for the rear wheel (rear suspension).

Suspension fork with cantilever brakes on a mountain bike

For a mountain bike, suspension is a great benefit, and some would argue mandatory. It keeps the wheels in contact with the ground more often, so the bike isn't bouncing off the ground over rough, rocky terrain. This helps with traction, and thus braking and safety. Bikes with suspension are also more comfortable and faster to ride, since fewer impacts need to be taken by the knees and arms of the rider and fewer small obstacles need to be avoided.

The drawback to suspension is pedaling efficiency. While designs get better every day, and many shocks come with a "lock-out" feature, generally when you pedal hard on a suspension bike, as you would during a flat-land ride or a climb, you lose some percentage of your pedaling force to the bobbing of the suspension. Even with a lock-out feature, which makes the bike rigid when necessary for efficient climbing, you still carry the extra weight of the suspension system around with you.

Many bike manufacturers make lightweight aluminum frames with cheap suspension forks, which end up being heavier, less efficient, and less comfortable than a steel rigid frame would be in the same situation.

Bike manufacturers continue to try to implement suspension on road bikes, from small shocks built into the top of a road racing fork to suspension stems and seatposts. However, for the city cyclists, properly inflated and sized tires still make the best option for giving your ride a little more cushion without losing other aspects of ride quality.

In general, it is a good idea to avoid suspension for city riding; it's not worth the sacrifices in weight and durability.

FRAMEWORK: AN IDEA GALLERY

Classic rickshaw

In this modified rickshaw, passengers get a front-row seat.

A perfect way to spend a spring day

A bicycle sound system in the front triangle, complete with input for an MP3 player or electric guitar, and knobs for volume and tone.

Old school, classic, and heavy-framed bike

With this braze-on feature, standing tricks become possible, and the handlebars are even more within reach.

Commuting in style on a bike that is one part big wheel, one part scooter

CHAPTER 8: TIRES, TUBES, AND WHEELS

The tires are ideally the only contact your bicycle has with the ground, so be sure and pay attention to them.

TIRE COMPONENTS

The smaller your contact patch (the area of your tire that contacts the road) the less rolling resistance your tire has. So, as your tire gets wider and wider, it becomes harder and harder to pedal the same distance on the same bicycle. On the flip side, as a tire becomes wider, it also holds more air, which provides more cushion for impacts.

Road bike tires tend to be narrow, with little or no tread on them, whereas on mountain bikes and cruisers they tend to be much wider. Mountain bike tires have knobs on their surface to create traction on loose surfaces such as dirt and gravel. Ideally on a road bike you are riding on a smoothly paved surface and the biggest impacts you are taking on your tire are potholes or the occasional curb (see curb-hopping techniques on page 40).

A couple of different tire treads

The common clincher tire is made up of three parts: a wire bead, a fabric core (sometimes called the last), and a rubber coating on top.

The wire bead is a piece of wire running along the edge of the tire that allows the tire to "hook" onto your rim, providing a secure connection, "clinching" the tire to the rim, hence the name clincher. The wire bead is also what gives some tires a circular shape even when not mounted to a bicycle wheel. Kevlar bead tires (made out of the same material as bulletproof vests) are easy to identify because they can be folded: the Kevlar bead is flexible and does not hold its shape like a wire bead does.

The fabric core gives a tire most of its riding characteristics, most noticeable in how a bike handles through a turn. Just like with cotton bed sheets, with fabric core, what you are looking for is the highest thread count. Originally made from cotton and silk, most tire fabric has been made of nylon and other

polymers since the 1960s. Higher thread count tires use thinner threads (which may be seen through the sidewall of the tire if the rubber is thin or clear), which make the tire more flexible, giving it a rounder profile and allowing for smoother cornering. When you corner, you lean the bike onto the side of the tires, and you really feel a smoothly rounded tire as you ease into and out of curves.

The rubber coating on the tire provides traction on various road surfaces, along with the tread pattern, if there is any. Traction is created by two factors: the size and shape of the tread and the hardness of the rubber. Softer rubber is stickier and provides better traction on the road, but also tends to wear faster, requiring more frequent tire replacement. Harder rubber lasts much longer, but doesn't stick as well to the road. Some bicycle tires also have a Kevlar belt around the center of the tire for puncture protection. If you are a daily city rider, it makes more sense to get harder tires (usually sold under a "touring" or "city" name) instead of softer "racing" tires, which you will wear through much too quickly.

Many modern tires use two different types of rubber, harder in the middle (which is used when riding straight ahead, and traction is less important) and softer on the sides (used when cornering, when traction is more important).

The tread pattern only lends more traction in wet situations; in dry situations it actually hurts traction because you have less rubber in direct contact with the road surface. This is why racing bicycles use completely slick tires. Because of the dynamics of cycling, not much tread is needed to effectively shuttle water out of the way in wet conditions and create a solid contact patch.

When looking at the tread from the top, it's often possible to see a direction to the chevrons (the pointy-looking triangular patterns in the tread). In road bikes, it's traditional to keep your chevrons both pointing forward, while with mountain bikes you point your front chevrons forward and your back chevrons backward, when looking down at the top of the tire. This is a custom borrowed from motorcycles, but there is some argument as to whether it affects traction in road bicycles at all.

Cross-section of a tire

Hold the level perpendicular to the frame and twist the nut on the opposite side snug before closing.

QUICK-RELEASE LEVERS

Quick-release (QR) levers are one of the coolest, if least understood, designs in cycling. Invented by racer Tullio Campagnolo in 1927 in frustration at how long it took him to fix a flat during a race, QR levers allow a fast on/off for wheels and bicycle saddle adjustments.

QR levers are actually at their tightest about 90 percent closed; they "loosen up" a bit when closed to 100 percent. This brilliant design means that a properly, 100 percent closed QR lever will almost never work free on its own, since it would have to work itself tighter before working loose again, which is practically impossible.

It's essential to set up your QR levers properly. Hold the lever at 90 degrees to the wheel and hand-tighten the nut on the other side; no wrench is necessary. Once the nut is hand-tight, close the lever completely; it should feel difficult but not impossible and should not require any additional tools.

It is also a good idea to close your QR lever in line with a frame tube; this not only looks nicer, it allows you to grab the frame tube when closing the lever and exert more force. It also makes it less likely that a stray log or fire hydrant will knock into the lever and flip it open.

EVALUATING TIRES

Cracked rubber on the sidewalls of the tire is one of the first indicators that the rubber is getting old, hard, and brittle, which means it provides less traction. If you take the tire off and flex it and the rubber cracks, it is definitely time to replace the tire.

While I am reluctant to recycle anything before every last iota of usefulness has been extracted from it, riding old tires can be dangerous, especially in a city where losing traction and falling could place you in the path of any number of vehicles.

It's also important to evaluate your tire in terms of the type of riding you will be doing. If you live in a rainy city, completely slick racing tires, which lack the chevrons to spread water out of the way, might not be the best choice. Instead, choose a tire with deeper treads. Knobs on a tire are designed for off-road

traction and slow down street riding, so if you are only planning to ride on the street you might want to switch out your knobby tires for something smoother.

Hybrid tires are designed with a slick patch in the middle for straight riding, but with knobs on the side for traction during turning, which is where you really need it. While not ideal for a dedicated mountain bike (off road you really need knobs in the middle to get good purchase on dirt and be able to climb well without slipping), they are great for a mixed-use bike that will see on- and off-road action.

A worn-out tire

THE ONLY PLACE I WANT TO LOSE WEIGHT IS MY WHEELS

You will hear a lot of discussion among certain groups in the cycling community about saving bicycle weight and building the lightest bike possible. This tends to be pretty expensive and involve complicated materials such as carbon fiber, Scandium, or titanium.

While saving 10 pounds (4.5 kg) of bicycle weight can make a significant difference in your ride, shaving that final pound (0.45 kg) or two off the weight of the bike may cost a tremendous amount without offering much noticeable benefit.

The major exception to that idea is with wheels. This is one area where extra money spent on quality and lightweight materials tends to pay off in ease of riding and speed. Because the wheel spins on its axis, wheel components travel p (approximately 3.14) times as far as the rest of your bicycle, so you get p times the benefit in terms of how easy it feels to pedal your bicycle. While you may not need boutique wheels, spending a little extra for Kevlar bead tires and aluminum double-wall rims is almost always worth it, and has an immediate impact on speed and ease of riding.

While it's a bit tricky changing a tire with a Kevlar bead for the first time because it doesn't naturally hold a circular shape, so it has to be massaged onto the wheel, it is a worthwhile upgrade for your ride. You'll instantly notice an increase in speed due to the light weight. Unfortunately, it doesn't make your wheels bulletproof.

CLINCHERS VS. TUBULARS VS. TUBELESS

Also called sew-ups or lace-ups, tubulars do not use a bead to hold the tire onto the rim. Instead, the tire is sewn around the inner tube and glued to the rim. These types of tires require a special flat rim, without the hooks to hold onto the bead.

Tubulars have several advantages. They are lighter weight than clinchers, though Kevlar bead clinchers come close to being as light; they have a much higher tire pressure; and they suffer fewer pinch flats because of the higher pressure and the flat profile of the rim.

However, changing a tubular once it gets flat is much more difficult. As a general practice, you need to keep a complete spare tubular tire with you, and you need to glue it to your rim, which makes tubulars difficult to change in the field and so impractical for city riding and commuting. There are people who ride tubulars in the city, or on tour, but for the most part they are restricted to racing.

Tubeless tires have become more popular among mountain bikers in the last several years. Using special tires and rims specifically designed to work with the tubeless system, they forgo tubes by having a stronger connection between the rim and the tire. This prevents pinch flats of the inner tube because there is nothing to pinch. It also allows lower tire pressure, which creates a larger contact patch on the ground and more traction, which makes it more attractive for mountain bikers; however, it's unlikely to transfer over to road cyclists anytime soon. There isn't much weight savings because the tire wall and bead are thicker to make up for the lack of a tube, and road cyclists tend to prefer more pressure, not less.

Cross-section of a tubular tire

INNER TUBES

The inner tube is a doughnut of rubber that holds the air inside of the tire with a valve for inflation. If you fill an inner tube when it's not inside a tire, it will blow up like a balloon, stretching to many times its intended size.

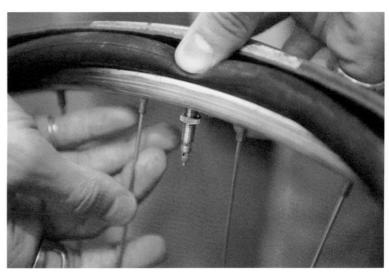

Be sure to screw the locknut down completely on presta valve tires.

There are two common valve types in inner tubes. The Schrader valve, often called the American valve (abbreviated A/V), is the same valve you see on automobile tires, thick all the way through, covered in rubber up to its threaded top. The Presta valve, sometimes called the French valve (F/V), is long, thin, and threaded all the way down its shaft. In the past thirty years or so, it has become the default valve of quality bicycles because it is lockable, so it leaks less air and enables higher tire pressures. It also has a narrower stem (6 mm instead of 8 mm), which means that the valve hole (the weakest part of the rim) is not as large.

The Presta valve has two main drawbacks: You can't remove its inner assembly, and most compressors are built for Schrader heads. The compressor problem can easily be solved by chaining a Presta–Schrader adapter to the compressor chuck. The inner core problem is less of an issue for city riders; it prevents the easy insertion of puncture-sealing concoctions designed to immediately seal any small puncture introduced into the tire. Since these products tend to radically increase the weight of the tires by filing an area normally filled with air with a heavy slime, I would encourage you to avoid those anyway, as their drawbacks overwhelm their benefits for most riders.

TIRE PRESSURE

If you examine the sidewall of your tire, you should see a recommended tire pressure range listed in pounds per square inch (psi). A typical psi range might be 40–65 for a mountain bike and 65–115 for a road bike tire.

The tube fits snugly inside the tire before being mounted on the rim.

This range represents the air pressure that will deliver optimal performance for the tire. Below the minimum number, you are likely to get pinch flats, which occur when your wheel hits something big such as a pothole or a log. (The inner tube is pinched between the rim and the ground, sandwiched in the doubled tire.) The top number is the highest the manufacturer recommends that you inflate your tire. Most riders prefer higher tire pressure for road riding because it creates a smoother ride and makes pinch flats less frequent.

Rider weight and personal preference play a large factor in ideal tire pressure; the lighter you are, the less pressure you need for correct inflation. An overinflated tire is less comfortable and tends to bounce over rough surfaces, which leads to less contact with the road and, consequently, is less safe. Try starting with the maximum pressure rating; if that is too uncomfortable, experiment with filling it to slightly lower numbers. Even experienced riders still experiment with their favorite tire pressure for different road conditions and riding situations. Also, in general, you should put 10 percent more air pressure in your rear tire than in your front to compensate for the extra weight the rear tire carries.

INFLATION TIPS

Always use a regulated air compressor or a bicycle floor pump to fill your tires; avoid gas station air compressors when possible. Gas station air compressors are designed for lower air pressure but much higher air volume. With skinnier bicycle tires, which require much lower volume, it is possible to blow straight through the sidewall of the tire. If you don't want to invest in your own floor pump, most bike shops and education spaces offer public use of their pumps, and stopping into your shop from time to time to fill your tires is a great way to get to know other cyclists. However, a gas station works in a pinch.

Your tires lose about 10 percent of their air a week when in perfect condition. This is why it is common to find a bike you haven't ridden in a year or two with flat tires. If you fill them up with air, the neglected bicycle is still likely to be ready to ride.

Fill your tires once or twice a week to your preferred tire pressure—it makes riding a safe and more enjoyable experience.

HOW TO: FIX A FLAT

Tools required:

- **Tire levers**
- **Patch kit**

Optional:

- **Box or adjustable wrench (for bolt-on wheels)**
- **Sink or bucket full of water**
- **Paper money**

TAKE OFF THE WHEEL

1. Take your wheel off your bicycle in a safe fashion. If you have access to a bicycle stand with a secure clamp, hang it from that. While some repairs can be done hooking your saddle onto any nearby protuberance and hanging your bicycle, wheel removal radically changes the balance of a bike and makes it likely to fall from an unsecured position.

2. If you don't have a bicycle stand, find an area of carpet or a patch of grass and flip your bike so it rests on its handlebars and bike saddle. (If you really like your bike saddle, lay a towel under it to protect it from dirt or grime.)

3. Downshift the bike's gears into the smallest cog in back. Pedal the bike (with your hands) to shift the chain over to the smallest cog.

4. Disconnect the tension on your brakes. For road bikes there is often a switch built into either the brake lever or the brake itself; on mountain bikes you generally remove a cable from its yoke.

5. If your wheel is a bolt-on, loosen the nuts but do not remove them; the wheel can come off with the nuts on, and leaving them on makes it less likely for the nuts to get lost. If it is a quick release, open the quick release.

Once you have the wheel off the frame, examine the outside of the tire for any indication of what might have created your flat. Obvious culprits could be giant thorns, chunks of glass, or rips in the sidewall of the tire.

It is considered a nice aesthetic touch to align your tire label with your valve, on the drive side of your bike. This can sometimes help you figure out what caused the flat in a tire, by being able to track how the tire and tube line up to each other, but is more often simply a sign of craftsmanship.

REMOVE THE TIRE

Now it's time to remove the tire from the rim.

1. Insert the lever end of your tire lever between the rim and the bead and get underneath the bead, choosing a spot on the tire far from the valve.

2. Pivoting on the rim wall, flip the lever over so that the bead of the tire is pulled over the rim. With a loose tire, which would be more common on mountain bikes, this will be easy, and you'll be able to then push the tire lever all the way around, removing one of the beads from the rim. With tight tires, it won't be possible to push the lever. In this case, hook the tire lever hook to a spoke on the wheel.

3. Position a second tire lever as close to your first tire lever as possible, and flip this part of the tire over the rim. It's generally possible to push this lever all the way around the tire, but if not, hook it to the spoke and use a third lever, working

your way around the outside of the wheel, until one entire bead of your tire is over the rim, and the other bead is off the rim, with the tire half on and half off.

4. Pull out the inner tube. Be gentle with your valve; where the valve stem meets the inner tube is the weakest part of your tube. To get the valve stem out of the rim, it is necessary to pull the tire back to create a clear path for the valve to come straight out of the rim.

REPAIR THE INNER TUBE

1. Put a little bit of air in your inner tube and start looking for the leak. It may be easy to find by running your hands around and feeling for air, but sometimes the hole is small and you need to submerge the tube in water to see where bubbles come out.

2. Once you find the hole, patch it following the instructions from your patch kit. The biggest mistake most people make when patching the tire is not waiting long enough for the rubber cement to get tacky.

If the hole is too large for your patch kit, or it is a rip or at the base of your valve stem, recycle your old inner tube and replace it with a new one.

3. Before replacing your tube in your tire, be sure to investigate why you got the flat. If the puncture looks like a snakebite, two tiny holes next to each other, you probably got a pinch flat from having not enough pressure in your tire. But if it's one tiny hole, be sure to line the inner tube back up with the tire and search the tire thoroughly to make sure whatever caused the flat is cleared. Be careful when doing so that whatever sliced the tire doesn't slice you.

REPLACE THE INNER TUBE

1. Once you have cleared the problem area, put your inner tube back on the bike. Begin by putting one or two pumps of air into the tube, enough for the tire to roughly hold its shape, but not overinflate. Then, pull the tire back from the rim and place the valve into the rim.

2. Next, tuck the lightly inflated tube into the tire all the way around.

3. Scoot the tube inside the tire over the rim. It's important to place the tire and the tube separately to prevent the tire from getting twisted.

4. Starting at the valve stem, tuck the tire bead back over the rim. Work in both directions at once with both hands, so the last piece you put on the wheel is on the opposite side from the valve cover.

The final bit may be challenging, but do not use your tire levers: you can puncture the tube by doing so. Standard thumb strength, and working patiently, is generally enough.

There is a special tire lever from VAR in France designed to help you get the last bit of your tire on. If you can't do it with your thumbs, you can use your tire levers, but never let them get beyond perpendicular to the rim. Lift the lever so it is perpendicular to the rim (or parallel to the ground if the tire is upright) and push the bead over; this will make a pinch flat less likely, though not impossible.

5. Once your bead is back on, fill the tire to the desired pressure, paying attention for bulges; if the wire bead isn't set properly, a section of the tire might bulge out. Inspect all the way around once you have filled your tire to ensure that the bead is properly seated on the rim. If it is not, your tire might not be compatible with your rim.

CASH FIX

If there is a small rip in the sidewall of your tire, it might not mean the end of your tire. If you fold up a piece of paper money, which is actually made of fabric, and tuck it between the inner tube and tire, this can reinforce the torn fabric and prevent the inner tube from protruding. Although this is recommended only for short-term fixes to get you to a shop to buy a new tire, I've been riding a front tire with a lucky bill folded up in it for four years without incident.

TIRE SIZES

The most common sizes for bicycle tires are 26" for mountain and 27" and 700C for road. These measurements refer to the outside diameter of a tire when fully inflated; however, for a variety of reasons, the industry now uses a far more useful size, referred to as bead seat diameter (or BSD).

BSD measures the diameter of the circle at the point where the bead of the tire seats itself on the rim. In this system, 26" mountain bike tires are 559, and 700C road bikes are 622.

The confusion comes in with a variety of leftover bicycle tire sizes from before industry standardization. Decimal tire sizes (26 x 1.75) won't interchange with fractions (26 x 1¾). But, as shown below, not even all fraction sizes are compatible with each other. (The second number refers to tire width; see below.)

For instance, most American road bikes from before the 1980s are 27", or 630 BSD. This is close enough for the same inner tubes to fit as 622 BSD (700C)—because they stretch to fit the bigger 27"—but different enough that tires don't interchange.

If you have an older bike, be sure to check its tire size carefully; there are a wide variety of tire sizes that seem compatible but aren't. For instance, 26 x 1 for a special form of racing bike called a "tri-bike" (designed for triathlons) has a BSD of 571; 26 x 1⅜ tires from Schwinn (S-6) is 597; and 26 x 1⅜ from a 3-speed or department store bike is 590. If you just read the sidewall, see that it says 26" and go buy some new 26" mountain bike tires (559), they won't fit.

It used to be very hard to find good tires for a 27" (630 BSD) wheel. However, when gas prices spiked in 2007, many people decided to dust off their old 1970s road bikes from their garage and found they needed new tires. For a few months, 27" tires were sold out everywhere, from bike shops up to distributors and factories. In response, many tire companies released 27" versions of their modern tires, alleviating the problem.

The other number refers to tire width; a 700C x 38 is wider than a 700C x 23. Tire width is a preference, as skinnier tires tend to be faster with less rolling resistance and wider tires tend to be more comfortable. Be sure to check that your frame has clearance room if you decide to switch to wider tires on your bike.

WHEEL COMPONENTS

The tire and tube on your bicycle rest on a wheel, which is made up of three basic parts. The rim is the metal hoop that attaches directly to the tire, the spokes run from the rim to the center of the wheel, and the hub contains the bearing assembly that allows the wheel to spin.

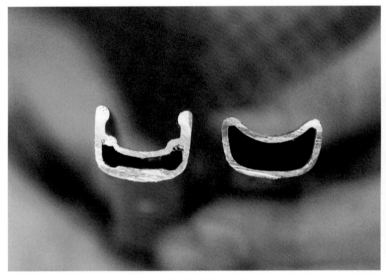

Cross-section of rims: hooked, left; tubular, right

While there are a great variety of alternative wheels made with composite materials and nonadjustable spokes, the classic spoked wheel is still the most common and most effective wheel choice.

The spoked wheel is so common that replacement parts are widely available. Each individual spoke is adjustable so that as your wheel gets a little dinged and dented (it does bounce around on the ground, after all), it can be easily and quickly adjusted back into shape.

Rims are available in either clincher or tubular varieties; the clinchers have a hook around the outside to allow them to catch onto the bead of clincher tires, while tubulars are flat in order to accept glue-on tires. Rims are commonly available in single wall or double wall; double wall are stronger and often lighter and are preferred.

Spokes are hooked at one end, generally to attach to the hub flange, and threaded on the other in order to be threaded into nipples, which are small mushroom-shaped threaded bolts that hang from the rim. Spoke thickness is measured in gauge; some common gauges are 1.6, 1.8, and 2.0, with the larger numbers referring to thicker spokes. Although thinner spokes make your wheel lighter, they can make the wheel less durable. For daily city riding, 2-gauge spokes are great.

Spokes are also available butted and bladed. Butted spokes are thicker at the edges where the spoke connects to the hub or the rim and needs the thickness for strength, and then thin through the middle. Bladed spokes have been flattened into blades in order to be more aerodynamic. Both of these offer benefits for racing wheels at the sacrifice of some durability.

Hubs consist of a shell that serves as the cups for your bearings, a rotating axle that generally has the bearing cones attached to it, and flanges that stick up from the shell body for the spokes to attach to.

Wheels are available in a variety of spoke counts, commonly in units of four. Thirty-six-spoke wheels are very common for their high durability, but 32- and 28-spoke wheels have grown increasingly popular for their lighter weight, though they are less durable.

Spokes can also be arranged in various patterns on their journey from the hub to the rim. The most common pattern is three-cross, which means a spoke crosses paths with three other spokes on its way to the rim. This creates a solid amount of lateral strength in the wheel in addition to holding the rim in good position.

The rim is designed to sit perfectly round with the hub at the exact middle, suspended by the tension of the spokes. However, as you ride, your spoke tension often subtly shifts, and your wheel goes "out of true," meaning small parts of the rim move to one side or the other and the rim is no longer perfectly straight. Your wheel can also go "out of round," which means it develops a flat spot somewhere on its circumference. If your wheel is "out of dish" that means the entire rim has moved to one side or another on the hub; this rarely happens on the road, and is usually a result of changing your bike's setup, discussed in chapter 14.

While it's outside the scope of this book, building a wheel is something almost anybody can do in about three hours. If you are looking for more information, *The Bicycle Wheel*, by Jobst Brandt, is an entire book devoted to just how cool the bicycle wheel is.

HOW-TO: TRUE A WHEEL

Truing your wheel is the process of subtly adjusting the nipple tension in order to ensure that your wheel is in proper true, with no side-to-side deviations. Bike shops have truing stands that allow us to dial wheels into nearly perfect true quickly and efficiently.

Unfortunately, a lot of the time you are out for a long ride and your wheel subtly works itself out of true and starts rubbing against the brakes midway through your ride, leaving you at a loss.

If you have the correctly sized nipple wrench, you can perform a quick wheel truing in the field and keep riding for the day. There are nipple multi-wrenches on the market that come with a variety of sizes of wrench built in; these can be useful to have with you on group rides, or to help you identify which nipple wrench fits your specific size spokes.

1. Find a grassy spot or put a rag on your saddle and flip your bike over so that it sits on its handlebars and saddle. If your handlebars are too narrow, you might need to lean it against something.

2. Looking closely at your brake pads, slowly spin the wheel to see where it hits the brake pads. The wheel should spin freely in your hands, then develop a bit of drag where the wheel is out of true.

3. Once you have identified the out-of-true area, identify how many spokes are in that area.

4. Squeeze together pairs of spokes in the out-of-true area to see if any of the spokes have broken or lost their tension entirely. In order to have a good baseline for what this should feel like, you might want to squeeze together spokes on a true wheel.

5. If you have a broken spoke, you will need to replace it, which isn't ideally done in the field. However, you can do a spot true around it for the ride home.

A wheel in a truing stand

6. If you have a loose spoke that isn't broken, try tightening it first. You do this by putting the nipple wrench on the nipple and tightening. Nipples are righty-tighty, lefty-loosey (right-hand thread), but it is often difficult to orient yourself to remember which way is correct. The trick I suggest is to picture a jar; if you held a jar in the same position as the spoke (often with the top down toward the ground), which way would you twist for righty-tighty?

7. Once you have tightened any spokes that have radically lost their tension, is the wheel closer to true? Spoke tension is often checked by the musically inclined by plucking spokes and listening to their note; by comparing the notes of various spokes, their tension relative to each other can found. It's important to remember that tension is only a starting point, and a perfectly trued wheel won't always have perfectly even tension on every spoke.

8. Slowly move the rim back and forth against the brake pad, and identify the range of the out-of-true section. Using the nipple wrench, slowly loosen the nipples of the spokes that go to the same side of the hub as the brake pad where the rim is rubbing, in quarter-turn increments, while tightening the spokes that go to the opposite side of the hub. This adjustment in tension will pull the rim to one side. It's important to match the tension, loosening to one side of the hub while tightening to the other. Otherwise, you can throw the wheel out of round.

9. Continue to spin the wheel back and forth in between the brake pads, slowly adjusting the tension of the spokes in the section rubbing the pad, until your rim no longer rubs against your brake pads. Spin the wheel to ensure that the rim runs freely.

10. Test ride the wheel. The full weight of the rider can often change the adjustment of a recently trued wheel, and often a wheel that is true in the truing stand loses its true within seconds of full rider weight being applied.

11. Lift up the bike and spin the wheel to check that true was maintained after a quick ride.

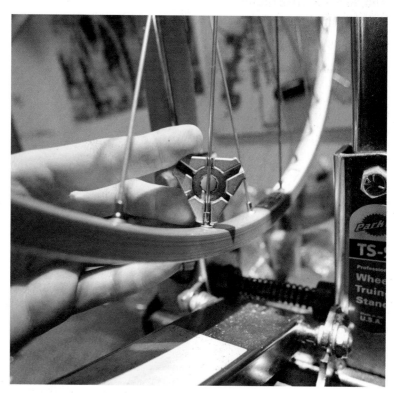

Using a spoke wrench on the spoke nipple in the stand

CHAPTER 9: BEARINGS AND DRIVE TRAIN

The drive train refers to the system of pedals and cranks, gears and chain, shifters and derailleurs, and wheels that propel the bicycle forward. Bearings, as discussed in the general mechanics chapter, page 106, are the little metal balls at the heart of any rotating system.

This chapter focuses on the most common type of drive train, the derailleur-based, multiple-cog, and chainring system, as discussed in the overview of the bicycle in Bicycle Anatomy, page 101. The general concepts here should apply to most common types of bicycle.

In addition, this chapter introduces bearing system overhaul, including working on hubs, bottom brackets, and headsets.

The hub shell serves as the cup in the bearing assembly; the bearing cones are attached to the axle. The axle is a long threaded rod, and the cones are held in place using locknuts, which twist against the cones to hold them in place on the rod without tightening them down on the bearings.

HUBS

The hub has two jobs: to hold all the spokes (as discussed in chapter 9) and to spin around its axle. The rear hub is where the gears are attached to the wheel, and your pedal force is translated to spinning motion.

FITTING YOUR HUBS TO YOUR FRAME

Rear hubs are wider than front hubs. Front hubs typically have an overlocknut distance (the distance from the top of one locknut to the other, the area of the axle that rests against the frame dropouts) of 110 mm, whereas rear wheels can have 120–135 mm depending on how many gears and when the bike was made. While adjustments are easy with a steel frame (but not with aluminum, carbon fiber, or titanium), they should only be executed under the supervision of an accomplished mechanic. When shopping for a hub, but sure to check that it will fit your intended frame.

Sealed bearings are becoming more popular in bicycles, especially in hubs. Sealed bearings have a weather seal that provides protection against the weather and longevity, making them useful if you live in a wet climate. However, sealed bearings cannot be serviced and must be replaced when worn.

GEAR CLUSTERS: FREEHUB VS. FREEWHEEL

Gear clusters can be mounted on your rear wheel in two ways, via either a freehub or a freewheel. The two systems differ based on their placement of the ratchet system that allows you to coast (instead of your pedals continuing to turn when the wheels turn). Ratchets are what you hear clicking when you coast; they are the mechanical element that lets the gears on your rear hub turn in one direction (when you coast), but not the other (when you apply pedal force).

With the older freewheel system, the cluster of gears is a complete piece, with the gears on the outside and the ratcheting mechanism inside. If you hold the gears and spin the inner section, it spins only in one direction. With a freewheel system, the hub is threaded, and you simply spin the freewheel onto the threads to attach it. The act of pedaling continually tightens the freewheel onto the hub.

Freehub systems move the ratchets into an assembly built into the hub, and the gears slide onto the flanged freehub. Freehubs allow bicycle manufacturers to place the hub bearings wider apart, closer to the dropouts, which makes for a stronger wheel, which is especially important in mountain bikes.

A freehub-style hub

HOW-TO: REPACK LOOSE BALL BEARINGS

Daily riding gradually wears the system down, leading to loose bearings. If your daily ride includes a lot of dirt, water, or impacts, the bearing system wears out even faster. You can tell your bearings have gone by spinning the axle with your hand and then pushing it side to side.

Does it spin freely, or does it feel "crunchy" to turn (i.e., do you encounter any intermittent resistance)? If it turns freely, push it side to side; is there any play or room to move the axle? If it is crunchy, or if there is play, you should repack the bearings.

With a good understanding of ball bearings and locknuts it's relatively easy and fun, though slightly messy, to repack a loose ball-bearing hub.

The only special tool required is a flat wrench. Though it is possible to repack your hubs with normal wrenches, flat wrenches help tremendously, and it is worth investing in one for the job.

1. Remove the wheel quick-release skewer from the hub, if there is one, and reassemble it with its springs. They are very easy to lose.

2. Remove any freely spinning axle bolts or washers and place them on your rag. This should leave you with a hub with your locknut on either end.

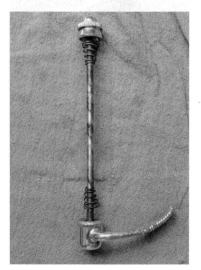

Arrange your removed parts on a clean rag, in the order of removal.

Removing the quick-release skewer

Many expert mechanics lay out a large, clean rag and place items removed from the hub on it in order, maintaining proper orientation (everything that is face out from the hub is face up on the rag, etc.). There are a ton of little parts in a hub, and it's easy to forget which way they were supposed to face, or exactly what order they are supposed to be placed on the wheel—no matter how good you think your memory is.

Remove the outside locknuts
using regular wrenches.

Gently remove the axle,
being aware that bearings might escape.

Bearing assembly before cleaning

Remove the cone nuts
using flat wrenches.

Remove the dust cap, if necessary;
many hubs do not have dust caps.

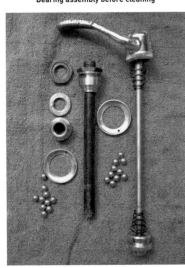

After cleaning

3. Pick a side of your hub, and find the right size flat wrenches to work on the nuts on your axle: the locknut (the farthest-out nut) and the cone nut (generally the next nut in). If it's a rear wheel, there might be a spacer in between them.

4. Hold the cone nut in place by gripping its wrench against some spokes, and use your other wrench to loosen the tension on the locknut.

It should work freely with less than a complete turn.

5. Spin off the locknut and any spacers or washers by hand.

6. Slowly spin out the cone nut, while simultaneously holding the axle in place with your other hand. There are free-spinning ball bearings in the hub, and if you remove the axle completely they all might fall out.

7. Slowly slide the axle out, being careful to collect and count any ball bearings that fall out. In many hubs the ball bearings are held in a cage, and only come out as a group once the entire axle is removed. Be sure to note which way the cage faces when you remove it from the hub; although there is no rule for which way the cage should face, it should be put in the same direction when you reassemble it.

8. Thoroughly clean the ball bearings, cone, and cup with a solvent such as Simple Green. Check closely for any pitting or damage. Replace the bearings if they appear damaged or worn.

Bearings are available in a few standard sizes; if your bearings are loose, you can measure them easily by seeing which hole in a spoke ruler (a handy tool available at most bike shops) they fit through. If they are in a cage, for the most part, it should be easy to identify a replacement set of cage bearings when you buy a new one.

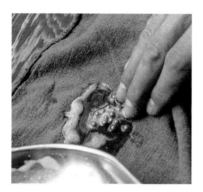

Place the bearings in a dish of cleaner or a dab of cleaner on a rag and rub them thoroughly.

Be sure to dry all parts completely.

Do not forget to also clean the hub body.

You can always measure your bearings for replacement using the holes in a spoke ruler.

REASSEMBLING THE HUB

1. Here is the messy part; using copious amounts of fresh grease, reassemble the hub by replacing the bearings, sliding in the axle (which should still have one cone nut and locknut assembly on it), and threading on the other cone nut. With a rear wheel, be sure to orient the long end of the axle on the correct side of the wheel, where it will be underneath the cogs.

2. When the other cone nut is threaded in, thread in the locknut. Tighten them against each other.

Using grease to hold the bearings in place, replace the bearings in the hub.

Replace the dust cap if necessary.

Insert the axle and thread on the opposing cone nut by hand.

Wipe off the excess grease. It will only attract dirt.

HOW-TO:
ADJUST THE CONES

HEADSETS AND
BOTTOM BRACKETS

Using a flat wrench to hold your cone nut in position, set the tension on the system using either a flat or normal wrench on the lock nut. Be sure to check the place with the wheel upright; it often changes the way the axle feels as opposed to being on its side.

1. Adjustment is tricky. Spin the axle: does it spin freely? If it does, push side to side and up and down on the axle. The ideal position for the axle is to have it spin freely with no side-to-side or up-and-down play. To achieve this, you need to slowly adjust the position of the cone nut relative to the cone nut on the other side.

2. Using a third wrench, hold the opposite cone nut in place against the wheel; this will hold the axle in place for you.

3. Loosen the locknut you are adjusting, and slowly turn the cone-nut in or out (in if the axle spins freely but there is play, out if the axle doesn't spin) a small increment; if it feels snug against the bearings, it's too tight. Tighten the locknut.

4. Remove the wrenches and spin the axle, checking again for play.

5. Repeat the process until the ideal cone nut positioning is found. Often this requires adjustments as small as one-eighth of a turn.

6. Once the ideal adjustment is found on the bench, mount the wheel on a bicycle and ride to ensure the ideal adjustment still applies in the real world of riding.

HEADSETS AND BOTTOM BRACKETS

Once you have adjusted a hub, you will find that the headset and the bottom bracket are very familiar.

A bottom bracket shell in a bare frame

The steering system of a bicycle is so simple as to be almost intuitive; turn the handlebars and your bike heads in the direction you turn it. The headset is a bearing system that allows your fork and handlebars to rotate in the frame. The fork spins while the frame stays static.

Headsets have a much different job than hubs; your fork rarely completes a full revolution (unless you have a BMX bike), and at any kind of speed most turning is accomplished not by steering the handlebars but by leaning the bicycle, meaning that your headset seldom turns more than 5 degrees.

Bottom bracket bearings

Top: loose ball bottom bracket; bottom: sealed bottom bracket

Typically in a headset the cups are press-fit into the frame, while the cones are pressed onto the fork on the bottom and threaded onto the fork on top (this is sometimes reversed on top, with the cone being pressed in instead). Press-fitting means that the metal cup is pressed into the frame tube and held in with friction, instead of being threaded, welded, or glued in place. This allows you to interchange the bearing assembly when the bearings eventually wear out, which means you don't have to replace your favorite frame every time your bearings wear out.

The important part of a headset system is durability. Because it is the loosest part of the front end, it absorbs a lot of front wheel impact. You'll often see headsets with larger bearings on bottom (where the impact happens) than on top (where the bearings exist mostly for alignment).

Bottom brackets are the other important bearing system in your bicycle. Located in the bottom bracket shell at the bottom of the frame, your bottom bracket is what allows your cranks and pedals to rotate.

The rotating element of your bottom bracket is called a spindle. The cones are cast directly into the spindle, and you adjust the bottom bracket by moving one of the cups (known as the adjustable cup) in and out. The other cup, known as the fixed cup, is threaded directly into your frame.

DRIVE TRAIN

The modern bicycle drive train is a wonder of simplicity and efficiency. You flick a small shifter on your handlebars, the cable scoots minutely, a spring-loaded derailleur slightly changes position, your chain moves to another chainring or cog, and away you go into another gear more mechanically suited to your needs.

The purpose of the drive train is to keep you in the right gear for the right riding situation; when riding uphill, it's more efficient to be riding a small chainring in front and a big cog in back, while the reverse is true when pedaling downhill. If you rode downhill on the same gear combo you rode up with, you'd be spinning your pedals, unable to contribute any pedaling force.

Gear combination is measured in what is known as gear inches.

For gear-inch calculation, nothing is better than Sheldon Brown: www.sheldonbrown.com/gears.

CHAIN

HOW-TO:
LUBE YOUR CHAIN

Bike chains are made of a series of plates and rollers that spin around on your chainrings and cogs, pulling the back gears so that your rear wheel spins when you pedal. Your chain is one of the most important areas on your bike to keep lubricated; it moves quite a bit and rubs against a lot of other metal while being exposed to the elements.

Bike chains are made up of a series of plates and rollers that spin around on your chainrings and cogs, pulling the back gears so that your rear wheel spins when you pedal. Your chain is one of the most important areas on your bike to keep lubricated; it moves quite a bit and rubs against a lot of other metal while being exposed to the elements.

Despite being held together purely by friction between the pins and the plates, properly assembled bicycle chains have a tremendous amount of longevity if they are correctly maintained. The average chain has between 8 and 10 parts per link: two outer plates, two inner plates, two rivets/pins, two rollers, and (with older chains) two bushings. So a 55-link chain will have 550 individual parts.

As the chain ages, it can "stretch" in conjunction with wearing on the sprockets. This is why replacing sprockets and chains together simultaneously is encouraged. It's never a good idea to mix a new chain with old sprockets; your new chain will quickly stretch to fit with the old sprockets.

The metal doesn't actually stretch, but the pins wear down where they meet the inner plates, which creates more wiggle room and has the effect of elongating the chain.

HOW-TO:
LUBE YOUR CHAIN

Under normal riding conditions, it's a good idea to lube your chain every few weeks to a month. However, a ride in the rain or snow usually strips the lube right off your chain, so it's a good idea to lube up after any wet ride. Your chain only requires lubrication on the inside surfaces, which rub against each other and against the chainrings and cogs. Any excess lube on the outside of the chain is just a sticky area that attracts dirt.

There are a lot of different lubes available, and many opinions on which is best (some people say nothing is better than rancid olive oil). The most important thing with a chain lube is to stay consistent in which lube you use. Mixing lubes together on your chain can lead to gunky results.

1. Hang your bike or flip it upside down so the rear wheel can spin freely.

2. Turn the pedals to slowly move the chain.

3. Drip a small amount of lube slowly onto the chain as you pedal to keep the chain moving, making sure you distribute the lube evenly to all parts of the chain.

4. Pedal vigorously to ensure the lube is distributed to the entire chain.

5. Gently wrap a rag around the outside of the chain and pedal the chain through the rag, applying enough pressure to wipe off excess lube without applying so much pressure as to making pedaling impossible.

6. When finished, the outside of the chain should be nearly free of lube.

HOW-TO:
BREAK YOUR CHAIN

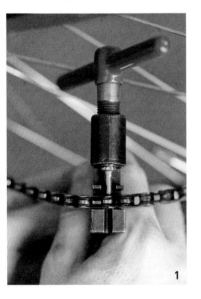

It's very simple to break your chain, to remove a few links, replace your derailleurs, or replace your chain entirely.

To do so requires a dedicated chain-breaker tool. Be careful; chain breakers are among the most delicate tools in the bicycle repair arsenal, and while it's easy to remove a link from your chain if you break it, it's very frustrating to find yourself stranded because you snapped the pin on the chain breaker.

1. Take the chain into the chain breaker and mount the rollers on the set of pins closest to the handle.

2. Slowly twist the handle to drive the pin into the chain, slowly pushing out the pin from inside the chain.

3. Stop before removing the pin all the way from the chain; the goal is to leave the pin resting in the outside plate of the chain, so that you can later reinsert it and reassemble the chain. It's not a disaster if you push the pin all the way through, but it's best avoided.

4. Take the chain off the chain breaker: success.

HOW-TO:
BREAK YOUR CHAIN

REASSEMBLING YOUR CHAIN

1. Place the chain back on the chain breaker; you might need to use a bit of wire to hold the chain together, or take it off the chainrings, if the rear derailleur is putting too much tension on the system.

2. Slowly drive the pin back into the chain using the pin on the chain breaker. Make sure it is lined up straight; any deviation to the side can drive the pin in crooked.

3. Once the pin is in, you might notice that the link is a little stiff; this is noticeable when pedaling, as the link will "pop up" when going through the derailleur or over the cog. It's counterintuitive, but to loosen the link press laterally on the side of the chain, push first one way, then the other, and this should free your link.

4. If you drove the pin all the way out, you have three options:

a. Add another link to the chain from an identically matching chain, or make the chain one link shorter, using the fresh pins in the other chain.

b. Use a replacement pin, which is extra long and tapered at one end, which is easier to push into a chain, then break off the tapered end once it is all the way through.

c. Use a master link, which comes with many chains when they are new and attaches without having a pin driven into it.

Correct chain sizing when putting a new chain on is very simple. Make sure there is enough chain that when shifted to the largest chainring in front and the largest cog in back (a position you really shouldn't use, since the chain is very crooked and thus inefficient and there are other gears that have the same gear ratio) the chain still bends twice when going through the rear derailleur. If the chain is totally straight, it is too short.

Then, shift to the smallest chainring and cog, and make sure that the derailleur still holds some tension in the chain. If it doesn't, the chain is too long.

SHIFTERS

In the beginning, all shifters were friction based. They were just a lever, and wherever you pushed them, they would stay put because of the friction. This required some sophistication on the part of the rider to find the right position; it was possible to leave the shift lever in a position where the chain wasn't ideally placed, which would cause phantom shifting (the chain hopping around) or noisy, inefficient pedaling.

As bicycles began to add more and more gears, friction became less practical because it became harder and hard to find the precise right place to put the shift lever, thus index shifting was introduced in the 1980s. This uses a series of click-stops in the shifter to move a precise amount of cable to put the derailleurs precisely where they belong.

Index shifting offers obvious benefits (precise shifting), but does have a few drawbacks. First, any cable-actuated system will slowly go out of alignment as the cable stretches and the housing compresses. This is no big deal with a friction system, because the rider compensates without even noticing for the slight change in adjustment. On an index system, compensation for this alignment change involves adjusting the cable tension. This is as simple as turning a barrel adjuster, but many cyclists fail to keep their shifters adjusted properly and thus end up riding with poorly adjusted shifters.

The other big problem with index shifters is that they require a compatible system (which would include derailleur, shifter, cassette [cogs], and sometimes cable) that all match each other not only in brand, but often in model and even year. For example 7-speed shifters from SRAM won't work right with a 7-speed cassette from Shimano, and some SRAM systems won't even work with other SRAM systems. There were a few years where the top-end Shimano shifters didn't even use the same cable thickness as the lower-end parts.

This is not a problem at all if you are buying a bike new. But if you are "crankensteining" a bike together from spare parts, it can become a major hurdle to find compatible parts for a complete drive train. When in a rush to get a bike out the door, it's often quicker to build a single speed or use friction shifters than to hope for the right parts for an index system.

HOW-TO:
ADJUST YOUR SHIFTERS ON THE GO

If you have an index-shift bike and you are getting phantom shifts (when you pedal very hard, the bike mysteriously shifts into a different gear), or your drive train is very noisy and lubrication doesn't alleviate the noise, chances are your shifters might need an adjustment. Adjusting your shifters subtly affects the cable tension connecting the shift lever and the derailleur.

By adjusting your shifters properly, you ensure that your bike will shift accurately and quickly.

1. Hang your bike, ideally from a stand, or if no stand is available, by hanging the saddle from a street sign, fence, or other protuberance. Be very careful when hanging your bike like this; it can easily fall off.

2. Shift down to your smallest cog on your back wheel. The same instructions apply for your chainrings, but will be discussed in terms of your cogs here.

3. Slowly shift back and forth between your first and second cog. Does it seem to shift too early (when you've barely touched the shifter) or too late?

4. If it's too early, loosen your shifter cable by slowly rotating the barrel adjuster on your shifter or derailleur. (Remember: righty-tighty). If it's too late, slowly tighten your shifter cable.

5. Continue to shift between your two smallest cogs while adjusting cable tension until it goes back and forth between the first two gears quickly and succinctly.

6. Test the adjustment by shifting through your entire shift range. It should improve the transitions all the way through the range. If it is perfect for 1-2-3 but then off for gears 4-5-6, or some other pattern, your parts might not be compatible, or you might not have perfectly set your 1-2 shifting.

To adjust your front shifter and chainrings, follow the same basic instructions above, with one exception: you need to adjust your rear shifter to properly adjust your front shifter. Your bike is designed to go up into its big chainring when your chain is toward the little cogs, and your bottom chainring when you are in your largest cogs, so you need to move the chain around in back to properly adjust in front. So, always be sure to adjust your rear shifter first.

HOW-TO: SET UP YOUR SHIFTERS FOR THE FIRST TIME

When building your bike from scratch, it's necessary to set the limit screws on your derailleurs to prevent the derailleur from traveling too far. Limit screws are small screws built into the derailleur that curb its range of motion. Since bike manufacturers want their components to be compatible with as many different bike setups as possible, derailleurs are deliberately designed to have a wide range of motion. Once assembled on a bike, however, the limit screws prevent the derailleur from going too far and knocking the chain off the cogs.

1. Turn the bike over or put it on a stand. After your limit screws are set, you'll need to adjust your cable tension properly.

2. With the cable tension loose (loosen the nut that holds the cable in place), find the limit screw that affects your highest gear on your rear derailleur, sometimes called your lower limit. (This is confusing, I know.) It is often marked with an H and is easy to identify because the derailleur will move against the force of its internal spring when you adjust that screw.

3. Crouch down to watch the chain roll over the cogs while you turn the pedals. Pedal with one hand, and use the other to slowly adjust the high limit screw until the chain naturally sits perfectly on the smallest cog with the chain moving smoothly from the derailleur cog to the wheel cog in a straight line.

4. Push the derailleur while pedaling gently up to the largest cog, and make sure that the upper limit is set properly. Be careful not to push the derailleur too far and knock the chain/derailleur into the spokes. When the upper limit screw (often marked with an L) is properly set, the chain can sit perfectly on the largest cog without being able to be pushed any farther.

5. Let the derailleur spring back to the smallest cog, pedal gently to realign the chain, then set the cable tension by pulling the cable gently through the derailleur and tightening the cable tension bolt with your Allen wrench.

6. Use the shifter to push the rear derailleur over to the largest cog.

7. Adjust the lower limit screw on the front derailleur so the front derailleur almost, but not quite, scrapes against the chain. This is also a good time to make sure the front derailleur is lined up straight with the chainrings.

8. Set the cable tension by pulling the front derailleur cable through and tightening the cable tension bolt.

9. Move the rear derailleur to the smallest cog with the shifter.

10. Shift the front derailleur up to the top chainring, and push on the front derailleur gently while adjusting the upper limit screw in order to ensure that the front derailleur can move freely to the big chainring without moving so far as to knock the chain off.

Once you are done, be sure to adjust your cable tension.

CHAPTER 10: FIXED-GEAR FIXATION

A fixed-gear bike is one without a ratchet system built into the rear hub to allow coasting. If the rear wheel spins, the pedals spin along with them.

In the beginning, all bikes were fixies. Fixed-gear bikes remain the standard for racing on a track, since the variety of gears offered by a racing bike aren't required on a flat velodrome and its light weight is a competitive advantage.

Fixed-gear bikes were also popular with messengers for their mechanical simplicity. Any bike that you put 40 hours a week on will need some adjusting, and with a fixie there were fewer things to adjust, meaning you could ride with nothing more than a 15-mm wrench in your bag

and mostly trust your bike would get you, and the client's parcels, where you needed to be reliably.

Sometime in the 1990s, the fixie crossed over into mainstream cycling culture as being cool, and by the 2000s there was a legitimate fixie boom going on. It has died down slightly, but they are still shockingly popular.

Pros: Mechanical simplicity, lightweight, hipster street cred

Cons: Only one speed, no coasting, hipster street cred

BUILDING A FIXIE: AN OVERVIEW

There is a distinction between a pure track bike made for track racing and a fixie, which tends to have more accommodations for street riding. To make a pure track bike, you need a track wheel and a track frame, which has an aggressive geometry and no brake mounts of any kind, because brakes aren't considered necessary on the track and only add weight.

For city riding, I recommend building a fixie and not a track bike, and adding a brake. With only a fixed wheel, you have only one braking system (your legs), and a good bike has two braking systems for redundancy. If your chain snaps on a fixie with no breaks, you're left to stick your foot into the wheel to come to a stop, which is a real last-ditch maneuver.

Bicycle drivetrain

A gear ratio of 46 x 15

A gear ratio of 44 x 16

A little dirty, this fixie wheel has a freewheel on the other side.

THE TRACK HUB

The heart of a fixed-gear bicycle is the track hub. In most threaded hubs, the cogs thread on in one direction and are tightened by the action of pedaling. However, with a fixed gear, there will be pedaling force applied in both directions, forward and backward, and it's necessary to have a cog that can withstand being pulled both ways without coming loose.

To overcome this, track hubs are designed with reverse threaded lockrings. This means that your track cog threads on righty-tighty (tightened by pedaling) and your lockring threads on lefty-tighty, so that if your cog slips at all, it will push against the lockring, which will get tighter against it. It's a brilliant and incredibly simple design, and is by far the safest way to build a fixed-gear ride.

HOW-TO: CONVERT A GEARED BIKE TO A FIXIE

Many people want to convert their thrift store road bike into a fixed-gear city rider, whether to save a little money or just for the vintage aesthetics of the older bike. It's one of the simplest conversions you can do. While a true track frame has rear-facing dropouts, like a BMX bike or motorcycle, and an aggressive geometry, other types of frames can be converted into fixed-gear bikes.

1. Choose your frame. Make sure it is a frame designed around 700C or 27" wheels, and most important, make sure the rear dropouts (where the rear wheel attaches to the frame) are horizontal (not vertical) and at least 1 inch (2.5 cm) long, though longer is better. Wheel position needs to be adjusted to maintain good chain tension, and long horizontal dropouts give you options as to where to place the wheel for good chain tension.

2. Purchase a track wheel, or buy a track hub a build the wheel. Please see page 165 for why you shouldn't convert a normal wheel into a fixed wheel.

3. Choose your gear ratio using the chart on page 164. The horizontal axis spells out options for your chainring, the gear attached to your cranks. The vertical axis refers to your cog, the gears attached to your hub.

A good gear ratio for a beginner to fixie riding is right around 80; too low, and the bike is too easy to pedal and your feet spin wildly downhill. Too high, and it gets too hard to pedal and you can't get up to speed.

As you increase in fitness, you'll likely go to a more difficult gear ratio.

Additionally, a gear ratio of 50 x 17 (a 50-tooth chainring and a 17-tooth cog) is the same as a 40 x 14, but the 40 x 14 uses much smaller gears and less chain, so the system weighs less overall.

This chart is meant to be an introduction but is by no means definitive, and assumes you are working with a 700 x 28C wheel and 165-mm cranks.

WHAT GEAR RATIO TO USE

		NUMBER OF TEETH IN THE CHAINRING														
		38	39	40	41	42	43	44	45	46	47	48	49	50	51	52
NUMBER OF TEETH IN THE REAR COG	11	92.4	94.9	97.3	99.7	102.2	104.6	107	109.5	111.9	114.3	116.8	119.2	121.6	124.1	126.5
	12	84.7	87	89.2	91.4	93.7	95.9	98.1	100.4	102.6	104.8	107	109.3	111.5	113.7	116
	13	78.2	80.3	82.3	84.4	86.5	88.5	90.6	92.6	94.7	96.7	98.8	100.9	102.9	105	107
	14	72.6	74.5	76.5	78.4	80.3	82.2	84.1	86	87.9	89.8	91.7	93.7	95.6	97.5	99.4
	15	67.8	69.6	71.4	73.1	74.9	76.7	78.5	80.3	82.1	83.8	85.6	87.4	89.2	91	92.8
	16	63.6	65.2	66.9	68.6	70.2	71.9	73.6	75.3	76.9	78.6	80.3	82	83.6	85.3	87
	17	59.8	61.4	63	64.5	66.1	67.7	69.3	70.8	72.4	74	75.6	77.1	78.7	80.3	81.9
	18	56.5	58	59.5	61	62.4	63.9	65.4	66.9	68.4	69.9	71.4	72.8	74.3	75.8	77.3
	19	53.5	54.9	56.3	57.7	59.2	60.6	62	63.4	64.8	66.2	67.6	69	70,4	71.8	73.2
	20	50.8	52.2	53.5	54.9	56.2	57.5	58.9	60.2	61.5	62.9	62.2	65.6	66.9	68.2	69.6

4. Choose your cranks, preferably shorter.

Many bikes come with cranks that are longer, more like 170 or 172.5 mm (or even 175 mm). However, on a fixie, shorter cranks are preferred, because with a fixie you have to keep pedaling through a turn. Since you lean your bike in a turn, longer cranks are more likely to hit the ground while you turn than shorter cranks, so city riders often choose 165-mm cranks for their fixies.

5. Assemble your chainring onto your crank (this may involve removing older chainrings already on the crank). This can be done with a wide flat-head screwdriver on one side of the chainring bolt and an Allen wrench on the opposite end.

You will need short, single-speed chainring bolts to bolt your chainring onto your cranks; the longer chainring bolts that come with a multi-chainring crank set will be too long.

6. Attach the cranks to the bottom bracket and tighten securely with the crank bolts.

7. Attach your cog to your fixed wheel by tightening with a chain whip, or a length of chain, pulling the cog tight.

8. Attach the lockring, which is reverse-threaded (lefty-tighty), using a lockring wrench.

9. Attach the wheel to the frame and size your chain by wrapping it around both the chainring and the track cog. If you cannot properly size the chain (it is either too long or too short if the wheel is placed in the rear dropouts), you will need a half-link, an ingenious device invented for this very purpose.

SUICIDE IS PAINFUL: SUICIDING YOUR WHEEL

There are some folks out there who promote converting nontrack wheels into fixed-gear wheels using a process nicknamed "suiciding" a hub.

This uses a metal epoxy and the lockring from a hub in order to tighten the cog onto the hub. However, since both the cog and the lockring are righty-tighty, if the epoxy were to ever fail, it would be possible for the cog to spin off backward, removing all braking ability from the bike. If this happened at the wrong time, it could be deadly, and I recommend against suicide. It is slightly more expensive to buy a dedicated track hub or wheel, but the prices are coming down, and the extra safety margin created is worth the price.

10. Set your chain tension. Many beginners overtighten their chain, in the belief that it will be more secure. In reality, this stretches out the chain, which leads to faster wear on the chain and cog. To find your ideal chain tension, pedal your fixed gear slowly and watch as it gets tighter and looser; this is a phenomenon known as radial oscillation. Find the tightest point in the pedal stroke, and gently swing the chain up and down. You should have at least ¼" (6 mm) of play in your chain at its tightest.

If you can't achieve good chain tension with the length of dropout you have, you can also use a half-link, which is helpful in dialing in the right chain length for your gear combination and frame size.

11. Ensure that the brake pads of the braking system properly meet the rim of the new wheel. While you can stop your fixie by slowing your pedaling or skidding to a stop, leaving the brakes on the frame makes a valid braking backup.

12. Remove the front and rear derailleurs and the shifters.

13. Brake check your bike, then go for a test ride!

FIXIE DUST

Fixies are the ultimate DIY bicycle project. For every bike lover, there is a fixie that suits their style and needs. Here are just a few ideas to get you started.

One of the original fixies

Fixies plus reflective tape: a match made in heaven

Freewheeling, freestyling

Fixie devotees know how to navigate city streets safely without standard brakes.

PART III: THE COMMUNITY

CHAPTER 11:
BICYCLE EDUCATION SPACE

Just about every day at the nonprofit where I volunteer, someone walks in confused about how we operate. "You mean, you're not a bike shop? Can I just buy stuff, or pay you to work on my bike for me?"

I dream of clients someday walking into a traditional bike shop and being just as confused: "You mean, I don't get to work on my own bike, but I have to pay you to do it?" For now, bikes mostly get worked on in shops, where you pay someone else to do all repairs and maintenance for you.

Bike shops provide a valuable and needed service, and there are bicycle repairs that people just don't have the time, space, skills, desire, or tools to do. However, there are an increasing number of DIY/DIT-style bike spaces cropping up

everywhere, where a different model predominates. These shops are places where people are encouraged to work on their bikes themselves and they are designed to create an educational environment to learn repair.

Nonprofit or cooperative bicycle shops promote the bicycle as a safe and effective method of transportation in urban environments. The ecological and fitness benefits of the bicycle mean that promoting biking is a public service to the community.

DO-IT-TOGETHER

DIT shops take a huge variety of forms, from nonprofits to co-ops to religiously affiliated organizations, but what they all have in common is a belief that with the right tools and a little bit of guidance, anyone can fix a bicycle. They may offer classes, one-on-one instruction, or just an open shop where people can come in and work. These spaces form the backbone of a new kind of cycling culture.

Nonprofit or cooperative bicycle shops promote the bicycle as a safe and effective method of transportation in urban environments. The ecological and fitness benefits of the bicycle mean that promoting biking is a public service to the community.

DIT shops have a wide range of forms, from nonprofits to co-ops to religiously affiliated organizations. What they all have in common is a belief that with the right tools and a little bit of guidance, anyone can fix a bicycle. They may offer classes, one-on-one instruction, or just an open shop where people can work on their own schedule.

While it is possible to fix bikes by yourself, it's more fun to do with other people, and you'll be surprised how much better you get at fixing bikes by doing it as a team and helping other people learn.

Typically, cooperative-style shops do not operate in opposition to but in tandem with for-profit, traditional bicycle shops. Both have a similar aim of promoting cycling and getting more people riding bikes. Generally, there is overlap of mutual friends, acquaintances, and a general sense of community. While official partnerships are tricky for tax reasons, it's very common at many of the shops to have a list of local for-profit shops to go to when a client needs something that the non-profit shop doesn't have. (This is often a daily occurrence and leads to more sales for the for profit shops.)

But in the even bigger picture, these spaces are the backbone of a new kind of cycling culture. DIT shops are dedicated to helping the cycling community grow, which boosts cycling activity, including sales at for profit shops.

LADIES NIGHT

Let's face it: The cycling world seems very male-dominated. One way to increase participation of both genders is to offer women-only nights at your community space. Its intent is vastly different than the purpose of a ladies night at a club. Many women (and many men!) find the male-dominated, testosterone-fueled atmosphere at bike shops intimidating. A women's-only night where women teach other women how to fix bicycles is a vital social service to the cycling community. It opens up DIY repair to a community who might otherwise be less involved.

HOW-TO:
START A SHOP

A quick Internet search for "bike co-operative," "nonprofit bike shop," or "bike kitchen" should give you a sense for whether there is already a bicycle education space operating in your area.

If not, start one! They are usually started up by a small number of people who simply decide they want a space in their area to fix bikes. Your city might even be large enough to support several spaces.

GROUP ACTIVITY

Your most important resource as you get started is the core group of volunteers who keep these spaces alive. The key to attracting folks, especially at the start, is to initially focus on the fun of actually fixing bikes.

Many new groups get bogged down with bylaws and meetings and planning, but the most successful groups try to keep it simple and focus on a shared love of bicycle repair.

Bicycles, especially old bicycles, can be damaged if you aren't careful, but for the most part it's hard to damage a bicycle such that it can't be recovered. It's difficult to fix up old bicycles, but keep going, and don't get discouraged. If you find yourself dealing with a particularly complicated problem, see if you can involve another mechanic in the space or find answers online that keep you moving on the project.

First, find available space (even if it's just a garage) and have a regular, weekly bike fixing night. Cook or buy some food, provide drinks, and see if a regular base group comes together.

Second, get tools. All you'll need is the basic tools we've talked about, and some way to consistently get the bikes off the ground. Purchasing a stand, which can often be picked up used on the Internet, is a great move if you have the space to store it. If you lack the space for a traditional bicycle stand, or the cash flow, a portable stand can be a great low-cost solution. While there are DIY bike stand designs around, they are often targeted at hobbyists who are only worried about fixing their own bike in their garage from time to time and lack the durability for heavy shop use, in addition to not being designed for the variety of bikes you'll face in a DIY space.

Then, expand. Once you have too many people coming to get everyone's bikes fixed in just one evening, expand to a few evenings a week. In the beginning, your core volunteers will probably get pretty fanatical, and show up for all the available shifts to fix bikes together.

Finally, gather educational resources. In addition to the mechanical instruction in this book, pick up a few other guides to bicycle repair. Have the Internet available to find resources. Never be afraid to admit when you don't know how to do something. A willingness to ask for advice from other mechanics, or look up relevant information in reference materials, is a strength. The desire to always learn new things will feed a friendly, cooperative atmosphere.

FINDING A SPACE

While a lot of groups start in a living room or a garage donated or loaned by one of the founders, a dedicated space becomes useful pretty quickly: Fixing bikes is messy, and there are a lot of tools to store and spare parts to be kept on hand. And, the space will take on a stronger identity if it is a dedicated space. For a volunteer shop to survive, a large group of people need to emotionally invest in the future of the shop and community, which is hard to do when its physical location is dependent on one individual's largesse.

Finding the right space can be difficult. It's important to remember that what you are doing is a great public service and there are often untraditional avenues to finding a space. A good bicycle education space promotes the bicycle as a safe and effective means of transportation with a volunteer workforce, and is often supported by environmental and social justice organizations at the start.

The Bicycle Kitchen, in Los Angeles, started in the kitchen of an empty apartment at the eco-village, a cooperative living space. Other shops in LA got started in spaces that were donated to them or rented at below-market rates, one in a creative warehouse, the other a storage space behind a retail facility. A nonprofit bicycle space in Memphis started in the basement of a church that had the space and believed in the spiritual benefits of education.

STORAGE SPACE FOR THE SHOP

One of the most important, and neglected, aspects of this space is proper storage. Depending on your operating model, you are likely to need to keep a large number of half-fixed bicycles and a tremendous volume of donated spare parts on hand in order to be able to help the wide variety of bicycles that are going to come in the door.

Even if a space doesn't initially appear to have enough storage room, don't forget to think in creative ways. For instance, many shops hang bicycle wheels, frames, or even entire bicycles from the walls or high ceilings in order to keep them off the ground and take advantage of all available space.

Defy gravity. If you will be hanging anything, remember that bike parts and bikes weigh quite a bit, and always drill into the structural studs of the space, never just into drywall.

All sorts of items can be kept off the ground, including using some plumbing pipe and a flange bolted to the wall, sticking out at an angle as a giant hook, to keep tires up and out of the way.

Many shops keep their tools mounted on tool boards on the wall. If you have multiple stands and tool boards, it's a good idea to lay them out identically, so that as your volunteers move from station to station it is easy for them to find the tool they are looking for. Color-coding your boards, and spray painting the tools to match, is very helpful, especially when cleaning up at the end of a shift.

Refresh the layout. My home shop does a reorganization every year or two over the holiday season in order to change the layout to take advantage of new ideas in how to best utilize our space. For instance, we were tired of people always wondering if we were a bike shop, but hadn't realized that our check-out area, which had a display of fancy bike parts just like a bike shop, helped to reinforce the impression. In our last reorganization, we got rid of the display case; fancy parts are no different from other parts and should be out on the floor with other used parts, we realized.

Be inviting. It's important to lay out your space out in a way that is inviting to newcomers. Fixing bicycles can be intimidating to many folks who haven't done it before, and a lot of times people are overcoming reluctance to come into your space and ask for help. An open and inviting space can go a long way toward making them feel welcome, engaged, and excited to get their hands dirty.

FINANCES

Even with an all-volunteer staff, education spaces have expenses and need a plan to cover those costs.

Even if you haven't gotten a nonprofit designation (which is discussed below), there are resources and spaces available to help you get started.

Donations welcome. One model is to suggest a donation in exchange for stand time in the shop. Stand time includes use of the tools, stands, and the help of your volunteers. This, combined with suggested donations for used parts and used bikes, can often provide enough revenue to cover the operating expenses of your space.

Build bikes. Some shops take the donations of used bikes and parts and build them into complete used bikes for sale in order to boost revenue. This can be very effective, but also means there is less focus on the educational aspect, since those purchasing the used bike are missing out on the activity of building it up themselves.

Offer (paid) classes. Many clients who already own bikes that work well are still interested in learning repair, and appreciate more formal bicycle repair classes. A lot of organizations run these classes on various schedules, charging fairly for them, in order to keep the lights on.

Fundraisers. Fundraisers are a popular option to keep the doors open. These can take the form of parties where you get space, bands, and sometimes food and drink donated and charge a high cover while letting the attendees know that it is to benefit your bicycle space. This can be a great promotion in addition to a great fundraiser.

Grants. Another common source of funding to support bicycle education spaces is grants. Although grants can be difficult to get, many are designed to support educational activities (especially involving kids), alternative transportation issues, and environmental causes. Cycling education spaces offer all three services to a community, and there are grants out there to support yours—you just have to find them. Hire a grant writer, or tackle the grant application yourself, with the advice of grant writing websites and books. It can be done.

BASIC NONPROFIT SHOP REGULAR EXPENSES

- Rent and utilities
- Consumables like grease and lube
- Tools, many of which are fragile and need regular replacement, such as pumps and chain breakers
- Tool loss due to theft
- Promotional materials such as T-shirts, water bottles, posters, and stickers

NONPROFIT STATUS

Deciding whether to seek a nonprofit status is a complicated issue. The primary benefit of becoming a nonprofit is that donations to your space will become a tax writeoff to those who make the donation, and generally lower tax rates apply to your operation.

However, many times smaller donors aren't even interested in receiving the tax writeoff. Many shops receive anonymous donations in the mail of old bike parts or sometimes even complete bike frames with no expectation or ability to create a tax receipt.

Larger donors will generally appreciate the tax writeoff, however, and the tax benefits for your organization can be considerable.

It is a lengthy process to become a legally certified nonprofit and it often requires the involvement of a lawyer. For many smaller bike spaces it isn't worth the capital investment and hours of work required.

You may find an umbrella organization whose own nonprofit mission is to provide nonprofit standing to smaller organizations that aren't large enough to stand on their own. These can be a great way to receive the benefits of being a nonprofit while just starting out, or if you plan on remaining very small for a long time. There are many organizations devoted to being umbrella organizations for other charitable groups. Community Partners, which can be found at communitypartners.org, makes a good place to start looking for one.

In most areas, to become a nonprofit you need to have a mission statement that must reflect a not-for-profit purpose—that is, other than making money. For instance, a nonprofit mission statement might be, "To promote cycling as a safe and effective means of transport" or "To educate local children about the ease and joy of bicycle repair."

RECRUITING, TRAINING, AND KEEPING VOLUNTEERS

It's a long-standing cliché of the business world that a company's biggest asset is its employees. If it is true in business, it's even more true for bike workshops. At its purest, it's the dedication, knowledge, and bike love of the volunteer corps of these organizations that keep them alive. It's vital to actively recruit, intelligently train, and work to maintain volunteers.

Volunteer recruitment will be toughest when your organization is new, but should be continued actively throughout the lifetime of your organization.

Comings and goings. The volunteer pool will always rise and fall, and your older volunteers will move on to new pursuits or get burned out.

Passive vs. active recruitment. Many groups rely only on passive recruitment (waiting for people to ask if they can volunteer), but active recruitment will always bring in some new blood. Post a sign in your space that lists volunteer opportunities. Reach out to the email lists of other cycling groups in your area. Talk up volunteering on area groups rides.

Many volunteers start with no knowledge of bicycle repair at all; all that's needed is an enthusiasm for bicycle repair and a willingness to learn. If your space has already organized classes, offering a free spot in each class to new volunteers can be a good way to pass on mechanical knowledge to them.

Community values. Every community is different, but the one thing they tend to have in common is a dedication to serving the bicycle community however possible, which is often very distinct from the experiences volunteers have had elsewhere. A simple training session, perhaps involving some skits for typical situations run into frequently by the volunteers at your organization, can go a long way toward communicating your organization's goals and working methods to new volunteers.

Retention. Keeping long-term volunteers is just as important as recruiting new ones. Regular meetings of your entire volunteer staff (monthly, quarterly, or at least yearly) to make sure everyone knows each other and is able to make decisions as a group are helpful. But smaller things that help make your volunteers feel appreciated, like throwing regular parties for the volunteer community or even inviting all the wrenches on a shift for a night out after bike fixing, can be done.

HIRING

This is a highly controversial area for bike education organizations, but many eventually choose to hire a full-time employee. While it's a point of pride for some to be an all-volunteer workforce, there are a variety of tasks that can be performed better by a part- or full-time employee.

Depending on your operating cash flow, you could pay for such an employee through normal income such as regular donations or through a grant specifically acquired to provide for an employee.

It's important to consult with a lawyer or directly with the applicable statutes on hiring someone to ensure that you do everything properly, including advertising the position if that is necessary, arranging for health and pension if required, and in general keeping your organization protected.

Having a large volunteer workforce and a paid employee is a delicate balancing act, but it is by no means impossible and can be a great way to aid the effectiveness of your organization in fulfilling its mission.

SCHOOL PROGRAMS

Many bike spaces engage in community projects such as earn-a-bike. This is generally coordinated with local schools, where underprivileged school-age children are taught how to repair bicycles.

They spend class hours repairing a bicycle and performing various other tasks around the shop. Once enough hours are completed, they will have earned their own bicycle.

The earn-a-bike program is a fantastic way to provide kids with bikes, but also gives them a sense of ownership of the bike. The mechanical skills they learn not only empowers them to fix their own bikes but also encourages them to realize how much in the world they can fix themselves.

There are many educational grants available that can help projects such as earn-a-bike as well, which can help keep these programs going in your area.

BUILDING A COMMUNITY

As cycling grows in popularity as a more and more valid method of transportation, the term "bike community" has become as nebulous as "car community." As in the auto world, where classic car owners aren't likely to hang out with drifters, there are diverse groups of cyclers in the universe.

There's always more opportunity to foster a sense of community within the cycling world. If cycling is just exploding, or about to explode, in your town and you lack any of the following ways to bring various cyclists together, you might want to create them yourself.

Online Tools

There are two online tools that are incredibly helpful in building a community for cyclists. If your community doesn't have them already, you should start them. If not you, who will?

Online calendar. BikeBoom (www.bikeboom.com) is an example of a very simple calendar that advertises all available, upcoming rides in Southern California.

Online user forum. A lively discussion forum community that is also locally targeted, and not just a local subforum of a larger cycling forum, is very useful.

Spokecards are laminated pieces of paper that stick in between the spokes of your bicycle. They are easy to make with laminating rolls from an office supply store, and they can be as simple or as complicated as you want. They can be made to commemorate a community event, and they are a great way to decorate your bike.

HOW-TO:
ORGANIZE A GROUP RIDE

If your town doesn't have a ride, consider starting one. The important elements are fun and regularity.

- Make a schedule, even if it's only once a month, and stick with it so that people know where to meet and when.

- Come up with themes and interesting routes.

- Ride the planned route at least a week in advance to ensure that all roads are open, safely paved, and appropriate for the ride.

CASE STUDY: MIDNIGHT RIDAZZ

Organized in secret and advertised initially through word of mouth and fliers, Midnight Ridazz is a monthly, Friday night ride (from 10 p.m. to midnight) with a different theme every time. It has a secret route map, distributed on a spokecard when you arrive. The secret route means that you absolutely have to arrive by the leave time in order to participate, which creates a fantastic sense of community as you ride together through the streets at night.
To keep the group together, riders can pull up to an intersection and politely block oncoming traffic so the pack of riders can continue through. This technique is called "corking." Although some drivers may get annoyed, once you politely explain that you are keeping together a small riding group, most drivers end up being very supportive.

A ride that starts with 40 people might grow in just a few months to more than 1,000 people. (If you haven't ridden through the night with 1,000 people wearing costumes, you're missing out.)

CASE STUDY: CRITICAL MASS

Occurring during Friday rush hour every month in many cities around the globe, Critical Mass is a bicycle ride that originated in San Francisco in the early 1990s.

It's not purely a "bike culture" ride. It's politically motivated, deliberately slowing down rush hour traffic in order to call attention to and agitate for better planning for cyclists. Although its goals are noble, it has the potential to turn off cyclists who don't agree with either the politics or the tactics.

A true bike culture ride should be welcome to anyone who rides a bike. Night rides, when the city streets designed for rush hour traffic are often nearly empty and when it is less likely that anyone is in a rush to get anywhere, can be filled with thousands of cyclists riding for pleasure without deliberately causing others inconvenience. Riding in rush hour traffic is not only dangerous, but it also deliberately gets in the way of lots of hardworking people who are just trying to go about their daily lives.

CHAPTER 12:
BIKE HACK PROFILES AND GALLERY

Sometimes, you want to do more than customize your handlebars or rock skinny slick tires on your mountain bike. Sometimes you want to go a little further. This chapter profiles some more elaborate options for bike modification. While some of these require more advanced skills (such as welding), small modifications can be accomplished with basic power tools and the ability to work with metal. If you've tried the stuff in this book so far, are tool savvy, and are eager for more, welding is not impossible to learn. Good luck and be safe.

Sugru-utilizing hacks

SCRAPER BIKES

Starting in Oakland, California, scraper bikes are decorated to extreme degrees, often in imitation of tricked-out cars. Aluminum foil wrapped around the spokes, in imitation of chromed rims on a car, is a classic scraper technique. Elaborate homemade paint jobs and candy wrappers from your favorite snacks complete a scraper.

Popularized by the Trunk Boiz and their boisterous YouTube videos, the scraper bike movement promotes cycling and a sense of pride in ownership in a community that has long been associated with materialism and fixation on high-priced automobiles.

Scraper bikes can be made in numerous ways. The wheels are a great place to start, since they offer such a large canvas for decoration.

SCRAPER WHEELS

1. Choose a color palette. While you could make a scraper with all of the colors of the rainbow, an elegantly coordinated scraper bike goes a long way toward establishing your sophistication.

2. Choose your material. While colored duct tape and polyester heat-shrink monofilm (available in hobby shops) make great materials, nothing beats recycled candy wrappers.

3. Wrap your spokes. Wrap your spokes with a candy wrapper, aligning it either horizontally or vertically for artistic purposes. When finished, wrap it in clear packing tape.

4. Choose a pattern. Create a pattern, often out of alternating candy brands or colors of tape. Once the wheel spins, alternating patterns create stimulating visual sensations.

Once you've scraped up your wheels, you can start to explore the decorative possibilities for the rest of your bike.

The wheels of scraper bikes are the perfect place to begin the customization process.

GLOWING BIKES

While reflectors in general make a poor safety measure when compared to emissive lights, especially LEDs, there is a great hack out there involving retroreflective material to make your bicycle, and you, more visible while riding at night.

Retroflective materials, popularized by 3M under the brand name Scotchlite but available from a variety of manufacturers, use glass beads embedded in the surface of the material to make them ultrareflective, reflecting back a much brighter glow than is normally produced by a plastic reflector. This material is used internationally to line the edges and lettering on street signs to make them more visible.

While it still depends on lights to be shining at you to work, and thus only works as a supplement to an emissive light, applying retroreflective material to your bike can drastically increase your visibility by making you a glowing ghost cycling through the night.

Precut kits for bicycles are available online, but you can also cut the reflective material yourself. Most sign shops will sell vinyl, self-adhesive retroreflective material in a variety of colors, though you might have to talk them into selling you less than the minimum order, since you won't need much; even a piece 6 by 15 feet (2 by 5 m) should cover the entirety of your frame with ease.

1. Stickers need good, clean surfaces to adhere to, so wash your bike frame thoroughly with soapy water.

2. Remove your chain and wheels. While this step isn't absolutely necessary, it is highly encouraged to make tape application easier.

3. Cut and apply the tape. There are a variety of patterns that you can create, including the pinstripe, the prison ring stripe, triangles, and stars; anything you can cut with scissors, you can apply to your frame.

Retroreflective tape can also be applied to your helmet, panniers, or shoulder bag to increase your nighttime visibility. Wheels and rims make a particularly effective area for retroreflection since their spinning movement helps their visibility.

Boarding by day...

....glowing by night.

Members of the Rock The Bike crew in San Francisco developed their own style of surfing cargo bikes. In addition to their double-take antics, they use The Down Low Glow, a Side Visibility light based on a small fluorescent lamp, to be seen at night.

CHOPPERS

Choppers refer to bikes that have been "chopped" in some way, generally to give the bike more character or otherwise differentiate it from the norm. A typical chopper might include extra-long front fork tubes or be a mix of tubes from multiple bikes.

Remove the screws holding the push bar onto the shopping cart.

While there are some mass-produced bicycles that reference the chopper style (most typically with an extra-long fork), these aren't choppers at all, since nothing was chopped; the bike was designed from scratch to look that way.

Chopper clubs exist in many cities around the world. They often have events, including workshops on welding and chopper bike construction, in addition to holding bike jousting tournaments.

Ryan McFarland, of Zieak.com, put together this fantastic design for a shopping cart bike. Simple to make, this bike is exceptionally useful for running errands with a heavy load for a low cost. All you need is a bicycle (preferably a low-end mountain bike), a shopping cart, and some zip ties.

A functional hack; half bike, half shopping cart, it's the minotaur of the bike world.

1. Remove bicycle handlebars. To do this, you will need to loosen the nuts holding your brake and shifter levers onto the bar and slide them off. Loosen the nut holding the handlebar onto the stem and slide it out. See pages 108 and 157 for more information on brakes and shifters.

2. Remove shopping cart pushbar. These are generally held in by a bolt at either end; you might need to crank the ends up with a hammer and chisel to get at the bolts.

3. Insert pushbar into bicycle stem. It should fit easily; pry open the end of the stem if necessary. Be sure to get the handlebar clamp good and tight.

4. Shave down pushbar to hold brake/shifter levers. This step is the most labor intensive. Any cutting tool should work, but ideally you would start with a rotary tool and then finish the job with a chisel.

5. Reassemble braking and shift assembly. You might need to use a flat-head screwdriver to widen the brake lever as you slide it back onto the shopping cart pushbar.

6. Reinsert pushbar to shopping cart. This will be a load-bearing element, so be sure and tighten the fastening bolts properly.

Replace your old handlebars with the pushbar from the shopping cart.

Re-insert the pushbar into the shopping cart.

Re-assembly of braking and shifting, along with some zip ties, completes the project.

7. Attach the fork with zip ties. Zip ties? Yep, zip ties. There are more labor- and material-intensive solutions, but zip ties work well to prevent too much side-to-side lean without restricting motion so much the bike becomes uncomfortable to ride. Remember, shopping cart wheels weren't designed with a human passenger in mind, and you need to build some suspension into the system.

Since the handebar/pushbar is supporting your weight, you want something at the bottom of the fork with a bit of give.

LOWRIDERS AND TALL BIKES

If ever there was an aspect of a bicycle that is best suited to personal expression and style, the height and length are it. Lowriders are inspired by the style of lowrider cars, which have been modified to ride as low to the ground as possible. And tall bikes evoke old-fashioned circus acts and acrobatics.

Lowriders in particular are decorated with elaborate paint jobs, excessive chrome, and electronically controlled hydraulic suspension, often with excessive numbers of parts. Seeing a lowrider with six chrome-plated sideview mirrors, a chrome-plated spare tire holder, and several frame tubes replaced with rigid chain is not uncommon. Much like their automotive brethren, lowrider bikes are less focused on getting anywhere fast than they are on enjoying yourself, and looking good, on your way.

Though frustratingly dependent on items that have to be purchased (unless you have a home chrome electroplating kit) rather than made yourself, the variety of tall, long, and low custom items available for purchase is truly astounding, and the room for personal expression (including airbrushing) is enormous.

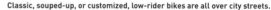

Classic, souped-up, or customized, low-rider bikes are all over city streets.

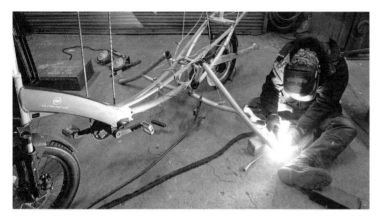

Metalworker by day, bicycle customizer by night. Jay Broemmel welds a mounting point for the retractable outrigger wheels on Fossil Fool's tall bike, El Arbol, shown below.

Fossil Fool testing riding El Arbol (The Bike Tree) in front of his driveway workspace in San Francisco. When used at events, this circus bike becomes a 1500-Watt Pedal Powered Stage and its rear branch supports aerial performances.

A tall bike is made by stacking one bike on top of another. An extra-long steerer tube is needed, and the chainline runs up to a bottom bracket off the ground instead of forward/backward, but otherwise it functions much like a normal bike.

While it would seem difficult or dangerous to ride a tall bike, it's actually surprisingly easy to mount it once you get the bike rolling.

There are many different designs for building a tall bike, all of which depend on what sort of bikes you want to stack and almost all of which involve welding, which is outside the scope of this book. However, welding is not that much more complicated to learn than anything else, and if you feel comfortable with the other repairs, building a tall bike might be a great next step.

A tall bike with fenders

Most tall bikes still retain the bones of the "short" bikes that are
stacked during construction.

BIKE HACK PROFILES

VILLAGE BICYCLE PROJECT

"We know that girls who own a bike get to school more often, and do better."

—Brittany Richardson, Village Bicycle Project volunteer

Bikes being donated to the VBP

Functioning since 1999, this internationally focused nonprofit is based in Vancouver, Washington, and assists in getting bicycles from the United States and Canada to Africa, largely Ghana and Sierra Leone, as well as providing bicycle repair education to more than 8,000 African students.

So far, more than 45,000 bikes have been shipped to Africa and distributed to people of all ages, along with more than 16,000 bicycle tools.

Trained volunteers spend at least six months in Africa teaching bicycle repair to bicycle recipients and others in order to help make the bicycle a sustainable mode of transportation. Volunteers also participate in their own communities. Local volunteers help coordinate the collection, repair, and shipping of containers of up to 500 bicycles to Africa at a time. Volunteering opportunities are available all over the world to organize shipping a container of bicycles from your area to Africa.

A typical recipient is Bismark Adjei, an eighteen-year-old photographer who has to commute to work in Elubo, the nearest market town, which is approximately 10 miles (16 km) away from his home. He uses his bike to go to work and for business calls. "I use my bike to reach the market when it is market day. Because I am a photographer, I need easy transportation so I can make my business calls. Before, I would have to pay 2 Ghana Cedis ($1.40) to go and come from work. Now I can just get on my bike and ride."

Recipients of bicycles using and fixing their bikes

PERSONAL NARRATIVE:
KABUL, AFGHANISTAN

"He's Al Qaeda."

"No, he's Al Qaeda. I'm not Al Qaeda."

In the way of teenagers everywhere, these boys standing at the roadside bicycle repair shop are busting on each other, about Al Qaeda.

Never having been to a war zone before, when I booked a cinematography job in Kabul I didn't know what to expect. I didn't expect the locals to be joking about Al Qaeda (picture two German kids in 1945 calling each other Nazis in front of an American reporter, for instance). I didn't expect there to be a huge party scene (there is even a lifestyle magazine in Kabul called *Scene*). And I especially didn't expect a city overrun with cycling.

Bicycles are everywhere, and nearly all of them are identical: Chinese-made PHOENIX-brand bikes, what might be called English-style cruisers. Their frames are made of lugged steel and have double top tubes, and they sport built-in pop-up kickstands, Chinese bicycle locks (which freeze the rear wheel to prevent a bike being ridden, but don't secure it to anything), and rod-actuated brakes.

My buddy who lives in Kabul took me to one of the countless bike shops that are everywhere in the city. Turns out one of the teenage Al Qaeda jokers was the trainee at the shop, with the old mechanic teaching him how to keep the bikes of Kabul running. My host, in Dari, let them know I was a mechanic and they instantly put me to work pumping up a tire.

The uniformity of the bicycles found in Kabul offers some benefits. There seem to be bike shops on every block, but they are mostly small, with a small selection of tools and parts. Because there is only one type of bike available, there is no need for the huge selection of tools and parts you see in the United States.

While we were in the shop, a man rolled up with a flat tire. The density of cycle shops in the city is so high that you don't need to keep a pump and patch kit with you; you just walk a few blocks and get help.

Without even removing the wheel (which is more complicated with rod-actuated brakes), the shop owner patched the flat in less than five minutes, leaving the client to pump up his own tire, pay a small fee, and be back on his way.

It's long been my dream to ride in a city that had more bike shops than gas stations, where I could ride tool-free because the infrastructure of the city was set up to support me. I just didn't know it would be in Afghanistan.

RIVENDELL

Rivendell is a specialty bicycle business selling custom-built bicycle frames and bicycle accessories centered around highly sustainable technology and a timeless sense of style. You might not always agree with all of their opinions, but you have to have respect for their consistency of vision and dedication to what they think is important.

Rivendell is very good at making you think about what really matters in cycling. Is having the absolute most expensive available part necessarily the same thing as having the best? Or is the best part or accessory the one that will last the longest, with the least impact on the earth, while functioning the best, even if it weighs a few ounces more than the top of the line? Also, their stuff looks classy and is likely to age well.

Rivendell was started by Grant Peterson in 1994 with less than $100,000 of investment and savings after his previous employer, Bridgestone, pulled out of cycling. Bridgestone bikes, and their elaborate catalogs, from the Peterson era (1984–94) are now considered cult objects by many for their mass manufacturing of sensible bikes designed not for racing for but regular, pleasurable riding over many years.

They currently publish the Rivendell Reader, a newsletter full of helpful information, informed opinions, and good old-fashioned folksy humor. If you are interested in learning more about obscure vintage derailleurs, or the history of lug manufacture, Rivendell are the folks for you.

BIKE KITCHEN VIENNA, AUSTRIA

Heavily hacked tandem locked up at the Bike Kitchen Vienna

Bike Kitchen Vienna, named after the kitchen the founders worked in at the small basement apartment where they got their start, is a DIY workshop space.

Volunteer-based and donation-run, the Bike Kitchen (BK) Vienna operates under the premise that those who can donate financially do so in a way that is appropriate to their income in exchange for parts and time. Those who cannot afford to donate financially are encouraged to donate in other ways, largely through work trade, such as stripping old bikes or cleaning and organizing the shop.

The BK Vienna has helped change the community of cyclists in Vienna, with neighborhood kids, who come to the Kitchen to fix their bikes together; summer celebrations with a bike ramp set up so bikers can ride into the river; and tall bike and chopper rides galore. They pride themselves on being a non-hierarchical organization with a biweekly plenum where the entire community makes decisions together, and they are a sexism- and racism-free zone.

XTRACYCLE

"What is the cheapest, lightest, simplest, most maneuverable, most adaptable, strongest way to carry cargo with a bicycle?" With that question, Ross Evans set out to design a better system for carrying cargo on a bicycle, a journey that lead him around the world interviewing people who use their bicycle daily in their business to determine the most effective way to modify a bike for cargo use.

The result was the xtracycle, an add-on that converts a normal bike into a cargo-carrying machine. Used on film shoots to hold camera operators, and used by surfers to bike to the beach with short boards, artists to haul canvas, and in countless other ways, the xtracycle is popular around the world.

The xtracycle's metal tubing assembly pushes the rear wheel farther back, requiring a longer chain. Its long wheel base makes it stable even when weighted. The extra cycle bolts into the area of your frame where the rear wheel normally sits, then the rear wheel mounts into the extra cycle. The most difficult part of the modification is moving the rear brake and extending both the chain and the rear brake cable, which is a relatively simple process that takes less than an hour, well worth the benefits of increased cargo capacity.

CHOPPERCABRAS

Choppercabras is a bicycle group devoted to chopped bikes that began in the late 1990s in San Fernando Valley when Paul De Gruen showed up for his regular weekend ride with his buddies on a chopper. His buddies, immediately jealous of the attention Paul was receiving from women, started building choppers of their own, eventually leading to the formation of Choppercabras. They are famous for their Halloween ride, where hundreds of chopper fanatics gather in costume for a ride through the night.

Choppercabras is built on a spirit of individual experimentation. Doing the welding in garages and backyards, and without the help of Internet forums and guides to direct them, they experimented and developed their own chopper designs through building and testing to accumulate knowledge.

"The best advice we can give is to really think the bike through. A lot of choppers I see didn't have much forethought, so you can't steer while pedaling without your cranks hitting your wheels, stuff like that." Other areas to really watch out for are chainline (keeping your chain straight) and fork rake. Too relaxed a fork/head tube angle and you get "wheel flop," too steep and your steering gets aggressive and highly twitchy.

ROCK THE BIKE

Rock the Bike is a collective of inventors in Berkeley, California, who specialize in inventions that push the spirit of the bicycle into the broader culture.

In addition to a pedal-powered blender available for human-powered smoothie shops and traveling smoothie making, they also produce their own cargo bike, and an awesome invention called the Biker Bar. This is a system that allows a large number of cyclists to band their bikes together and pedal to generate power. As few as three cyclists can be enough to power a reasonable-sized outdoor music concert indefinitely. It comes built into a trailer that can be ridden to a concert or other event with up to 250 pounds (113 kg) of other equipment stored on top.

HACKNEY BIKEWORKSHOPS

Located in the dynamic neighborhood of Hackney in London, where gated communities butt up against public housing and there is a thriving arts scene, Hackney Bikeworkshops has survived a tumultuous history. Starting with nothing, and losing two spaces before settling on their current shop, the shop currently provides a valuable service to the community, attracting up to twenty volunteers for a regular night at the shop.

GLOSSARY

29er Increasingly popular style of mountain bike that uses 622 BSD mountain wheels, which are the same size as road wheels. The larger wheel makes going over obstacles easier, but also is sometimes uncomfortable for shorter riders.

105 Shimano's mid-level road gruppo, one step below 600, common on touring bikes and very popular with the urban cyclist.

531 A model tubeset made by the Reynolds corporation, the most popular U.S. tubeset manufacturer. 531 was the prestige/racing tubset for lugged steel (countless Tour de France winners from the 1950s through the 1960s rode 531) and it has tremendous cult appeal, up to and including 531 logo tattoos. Insider note: It is pronounced "five three one," not "five thirty one."

600 Now known as Ultrega, this is Shimano's second from the top road gruppo. Still nice enough to get you reasonable respect without being too flashy, like Dura Ace.

Aero Many bicycle parts, such as spokes, come in "aero" options, which are designed to reduce air resistance and thus increase speed. While demonstrable results are seen in racing with aero helmets, frames, and spokes, the results aren't worth the drawbacks at city speeds. Those drawbacks are mainly cost, durability, and looking silly.

Allen Wrench Sometimes called an "allen key" or "hex wrench," this is the six-sided tool that most people associate with cheap furniture construction. Used all over cycling, it is worth acquiring a small allen wrench to keep with you as you ride.

Aluminum A frame material that grew in popularity during the 1980s; it is extremely light, but also stiff and unforgiving.

Bearing (ball type) A set of tiny metal balls that rotate within a cup; the ball bearing system is what allows your bicycle wheels, handlebars, and cranks to spin so freely.

Bar End Shifter Popular with long distance tourists and urban cyclists for their durability over integrated shifting systems, bar-end shifters are installed at the end of your drop handlebars.

Bead Seat (BSD) Bead Seat Diameter refers to the diameter of the part of the wheel where the tire bead connects with the rim. The BSD is the best way to compare actual wheel sizes and determine what tire you need for your bicycle.

Biopace An oval-chainring experiment of Shimano's in the late 1980s, Biopace provides great pedaling advantages to many riders by making it so you are pulling more chain in the "power" downstroke, and less when you have less power (the top and bottom of your pedal stroke). Brilliant, but causes most people knee pain unless their body is optimized for it. Biopace rings are not compatible with fixed gear bicycles.

Braze-on A fitting brazed into the frame, such as for the mounting of water bottles or racks.

Bridgestone A Japanese conglomerate that made very nice bicycles during the 1970s and 1980s, with a great combination of lugged steel frames made in Japan combined with smartly chosen components. "RB-1" (road-bike #1) was top of the line and still has some cult value.

Brooks Handmade saddle manufacturer in England.

Butted The process of varying the thickness of the tube wall for bicycle tubes to minimize tube weight. You can determine where these variations are by flicking your finger against various sections of the tube and listening to the sounds.

Cable Stop A common braze-on to a frame (or they can be bolted on later), they provide a fixed position for cable and housing to stop.

Cadence The rhythm with which you pedal. Higher cadence is considered more efficient.

Campagnolo Prestigious Italian manufacturer of road bicycle parts. Affectionately called "campy" by its friends and lovers.

Carbon Fiber Ultralight, directionally controllable material increasingly common in frames and components but prone to catastrophic failure without warning.

Century Riding your bicycle 100 miles (160 km) in one trip.

Chain Line With a single speed, the frame/component alignment that keeps your rear cog directly behind your chainring. With a multi-speed bicycle, the combination of gears that gives you a straight running chain. Once you know to look out for it, nothing feels as good as straight chainline.

Chain Hanger A considerate braze-on built into classic frames that give you a place to hang your chain when removing your rear wheel.

Chrome-Moly A steel alloy with trace amounts of chromium and molybdenum; it's the most common material for high-quality lugged-steel frames and forks.

Clipless Pedals Confusing name for pedals that use toe-cleats and lack cages to keep your feet connected to your pedals for power in your upstroke.

Columbus Italian bicycle tube manufacturer. With Reynolds, these two firms make most of the prestige tubing for the industry.

Cottered Cranks Old-style crank attachment system that uses a cotter-pin, which is inserted and held in place with friction perpendicular to the crank, holding the crank onto the axle.

Cyclocomputer A computer you can mount to your bicycle to tell you fun information such as speed, distance travelled, and sometimes even what gear you are in. It'll be stolen the first time you leave it on your bike in the city, so it's not popular in urban areas, but it's great on long touring rides.

Cyclo-cross A style of off-road racing with bikes that more closely resemble road bikes.

Derailleur The part on your bike that moves the chain from gear to gear.

Dura Ace Top-of-the-line, prestige road gruppo from Shimano. Very nice road parts, great "bling" objects, but also theft magnets and usually not durable enough for daily road riding.

Fixie Slang term referring to a road bike that has been converted to single-speed, with no coasting configuration, and often with brakes. Generally refers to bikes that have been hacked into this setup, as opposed to track bikes built from scratch for that style of riding.

Eddie Merckx Belgian racer with cult status to many urban cyclists who disdain the clean, corporate, and dope-heavy world of modern cycle racing (though he had a few dope controversies himself). Unlike modern racers who target specific events and cater their training year around to specific goals, racers of his generation competed yearround. In his career, he won the Tour de France (five times), the Giro D'Italia, and the Vuelta de Espana. Beloved for turning down one million Belgian francs from Coca-Cola to ride in the Tour in 1979 because he didn't feel strong enough to do both that and still win the Giro, which his team valued more. Went on to found the Merckx frame company.

Freehub Hub system in which the ratchets (which allow you to coast) are built into the hub. Freehub is a more durable and more modern system.

Freewheel Older hub system in which the ratchets are built into the cog set.

Friction Shift Shifting system in which the shifter is held in place by friction; it allows for minute adjustments and it is better suited for low-gear systems (such as 10-speed bikes).

Ghost Shifting When your shifting is not adjusted properly, your bike shifts from one gear to another seemingly unpredictably. A very easy fix.

Gruppo Italian term for "group"; refers to a matched set of parts designed to work together for a bike at a given price point and finishing quality.

Hydraulic Using fluid instead of cables, hydraulic systems are common on motorcycles and automobiles, and gradually increasing in popularity on bicycles.

Indexed Shifting In contrast to friction shifting, index shift systems have a series of ratchets that index stops for shifting. Great for gear systems with a large gear volume, such as 21-speed or 27-speed bikes.

Keirin Japenese track-racing circuit. Keirin parts are popular cult objects in the fixie scene. If you are the right height for a 55 cm frame or smaller, Keirin frames are popular options.

Kickstand A part used to keep a bicycle upright when not in use. By default, kickstands have been replaced by the practice of locking your bike to something whenever you park it. Thus, kickstands are mostly for cops.

Masi Italian frame maker who also opened a factory in Southern California in the 1970s and 1980s. The ultimate lust object for the hero of *Breaking Away* was an Orange Masi.

Mavic French component and wheel manufacturer.

Metric System International standard of measurements; common in cycling world.

NOS "New-Old-Stock" Old parts that have never left their box, usually unsold inventory from bicycle shops; the nicest versions of old parts are NOS.

Pannier Bags that attach to the rear rack of your bicycle; useful for both commuting and touring.

Pista Italian word for "track"; frequently used in branding for track and fixie parts.

Q-factor Refers to the width between your cranks.

Safety Bicycle General term referring to the double-diamond frame structure most common in cycling (as opposed to recumbents, tandems, and so on.)

Schwinn Chicago-based bicycle manufacturer dominant throughout the middle of the twentieth century, widely associated with the bike boom of the 1970s. Many Schwinn parts are incompatible with standard sizes in the industry.

Sealed Bearings Bearing systems that are replaced in a cartridge and cannot be repacked.

Shimano Dominant Japanese manufacturer and bicycle part pioneer.

Single Track A single-width trail for mountain bikes that is too narrow for other vehicles (which need double width).

Skewer The quick release system that runs through the middle of the hub axle.

Skid Patch Fixie riders who frequently skid to a stop will consistently wear out the same areas of their tires, since their feet are always in the same position when they stop. Different gear/wheel ratios create more or fewer skid patches on a tire; more is better, because it distributes the load. If you end up with only one skid patch, you'll eat through that patch must faster.

SPD Stands for "Shimano Pedalling Dynamics." This is the system of two-bolt cleats and pedals that is most common in the industry for clipless/clip-in pedals.

Super Record The prestige gruppo from Campagnolo.

Touring Riding your bicycle, alone or with others, for long distances, generally over several days. Why? 'Cause it's so much fun.

Trek Mass-market U.S. bicycle manufacturer; its early frames from the 1970s and (to a small extent) early 1980s still have a lot of street cred despite how dominant they now are in the market.

Track Bike A bicycle designed for racing on a track; they have aggressive geometries and rear-facing dropouts, and they lack mounting points for brakes, as opposed to fixies, which are converted road bicycles.

Track Stand Standing still while mounted on your bike, with your feet on the pedals, by gently rocking your track bicycle forward and backward. Popular at stoplights so you don't have to unclip or take your feet out of your cages. It also looks cool. A track stand can be done on a coastable bike if you are on a slight incline.

RECOMMENDED READING

Barnetts Bicycle Institute
www.bbinstitute.com
A major institution for professional training and certification, they also publish the exhaustive "Barnett's Manual" for bicycle repair.

Bike Snob
http://bikesnobnyc.blogspot.com/
A very opininated blogger with lots of great info. He's also written a book.

Brandt, Jobst. *The Bicycle Wheel*, 3rd Edition. Avocet, 1993
The most thoroughly researched and informative book on bicycle wheels ever written, by Porsche engineer Jobst Brandt.

Koichi Yamaguchi School
www.yamaguchibike.com
A school devoted to learning frame building from internationally recognized master framebuilder Koichi Yamaguchi.

Rivendell Bicycles
www.rivbike.com
Run by Grant Peterson, a man with a very specific vision for bicycles. Follow the "read" link.

Rock the Bike
www.rockthebike.com
Bike advocates pushing the limits of bike culture and spreading the spirit of the bike by organizing, entertaining, inspiring, educating, and inventing new ways to get the message out there.

Sheldon Brown
www.sheldonbrown.com
Boston-based authority on all things bicycle, with an extensive website full of information, and some thorough opinions. Often used as a resource when settling arguments and bets between cycle geeks.

Sutherland, Howard. *Sutherland's Handbook for Bicycle Mechanics.* Weighing it at 5.2 lbs, the Sutherland's Guide, along with Barnett's Manual, serves as the one of the most epic cycling repair texts.

United Bicycle Institute (UBI)
www.bikeschool.com
One of the premiere institutions for pursuing professional training and certification in all forms of bicycle repair up to and including frame building.

INDEX

ABOUT THE AUTHOR AND COPHOTOGRAPHER

Charles Haine has been a bicycle mechanic for more than a decade. He learned to fix bikes at a bicycle cooperative at Oberlin College, followed by stints in the sales department at several bicycle shops in his hometown of Washington, D.C., including Blazing Saddles and Citybikes, and time at both the Bike Spot and Bikecology in Los Angeles. He is currently the chairman of the Bicycle Kitchen, a nonprofit bicycle education space in Los Angeles, California, where he has also been a volunteer for seven years. He has taught beginning and advanced bicycle mechanics to the general public and to other volunteers at the Bicycle Kitchen to help them better serve the community. For a living he works in motion pictures. In his spare time he gets into arguments about how to properly address brake squeak.

Photo by Hilary Jones ©2010

Drew Bienemann was born and raised in Denver, Colorado. After graduating from film school in Canada, he moved to Los Angeles, where he divides his time between working as a photographer and volunteering at the Bicycle Kitchen, a nonprofit community bicycle education space. He hopes to one day own many large dogs.